TRAVELING THROUGH
ILLINOIS

STORIES OF I-55 LANDMARKS & LANDSCAPES BETWEEN CHICAGO & ST. LOUIS

LuAnn Cadden & Ted Cable

Published by The History Press
Charleston, SC 29403
www.historypress.net

Copyright © 2013 by LuAnn Cadden and Ted T. Cable
All rights reserved

Cover image of Chicago skyline courtesy of Fleishman-Hillard.

First published 2013

ISBN 978-1-5402-2168-1

Library of Congress CIP data applied for.

Notice: The information in this book is true and complete to the best of our knowledge. It is offered without guarantee on the part of the authors or The History Press. The authors and The History Press disclaim all liability in connection with the use of this book.

All rights reserved. No part of this book may be reproduced or transmitted in any form whatsoever without prior written permission from the publisher except in the case of brief quotations embodied in critical articles and reviews.

Mile 100. The Sangamon Avenue exit leads me back home. Just a few miles down the road, my parents, Mike and Mary Lou Aiello, purchased their home, raised three boys and one girl and still reside there today. All of my brothers and their families still live in the Springfield area. This is where my great-grandparents settled and worked as coal miners and maids. It is to all of my family who made Illinois their home in America that I dedicate this book.
—*LuAnn Cadden*

Mile 250. Exit eastbound on I-80, and in about forty miles, you will be in my hometown of Lansing, Illinois. Lansing is still home to my parents, Ted and Beverly Cable, and my brother, Scott, and his wife, Bonnie. Many of the research trips in preparation for this book were also trips home to see family. It is to these family members that I dedicate this book about traveling across Illinois.
—*Ted T. Cable*

CONTENTS

Preface	7
Acknowledgements	9
Introduction	11

PART I: STATE SYMBOLS AND A HIGHWAY GUIDE
Illinois State Symbols	15
Guiding You Along the Highway	23

PART II: SOUTHBOUND
Chicago	25
Leaving the Lakefront	27
From Chicago to St. Louis	29
A Fond Farewell	98

PART III: NORTHBOUND
Welcome to Illinois	99
From St. Louis to Chicago	100
Approaching Chicago	168
End of the Road	171

Bibliography	173
Index	185
About the Authors	191

PREFACE

The question is always asked by the curious travelers who have crossed the Plains at Interstate speeds, "How can you live here without the mountains, the ocean, the woods?" But what they are really speaking to is their desire to "get it" right away. The sublime of this place that we call the prairie is one of patience and looking. There is no quick fix...If one is to understand the beauty of this place, the old answers just won't do.
–Keith Jacobshagen, *"Personal Journey,"* The Changing Prairie *(1995)*

After driving for hours across Illinois on a field-flanked highway, minds start to ignore the repeat visitors to the eyes. Rows of corn and soybeans fill car windows as leisurely as lawns and sidewalks do along the road to work each day. Barns and grain bins move aside through the traveler's peripheral vision.

According to the Illinois Department of Transportation, more than twenty thousand vehicles travel Interstate 55 each day. That does not include the hundreds of thousands of people who daily travel the Stevenson Expressway in the Chicago Metro area. When these people describe their experiences driving Interstate 55 through Illinois, the words "boring" and "flat" dominate their stories. The purpose of this book is to change the drive between Chicago and St. Louis from being barely endurable to enjoyable.

Many books have been written about Route 66, but none has been targeted for the multitudes of travelers who drive Interstate 55. Our book mixes Route 66 nostalgia with sights and stories along the present-day modern

Preface

route from Chicago to St. Louis. Our research and personal interviews provide stories never before told to Illinois travelers about the state's history, culture, agriculture and industry. This book also interprets the rivers and lakes, as well as the plants and wildlife, seen along the highway.

We hope that our book will provide commuters a refreshing new perspective of the highway you travel each day. For Illinois residents, we hope this will offer new stories about familiar places and new places you can explore close to home. For those travelers passing through Illinois, we hope this is an entertaining and educational guide to the fascinating people and places across Illinois. Most of all, we hope that our book will help you find truth in the phrase "half the fun is getting there."

Interstate 55 across Illinois has much to offer if you truly see. Not merely look, but *see*. In the words of Marcel Proust, we believe that "the real voyage of discovery lies not in seeking new lands, but in seeing with new eyes." This is the essence of our book.

ACKNOWLEDGEMENTS

We would like to thank the many professionals, colleagues, Illinois citizens, friends and family members for their help in steering us in the right direction as we gathered information and photographs for our book: Brian Aiello (historian); Mary Louise, Michael and Phil Aiello (expert drivers who slowed, pulled over and probably broke some laws as LuAnn took pictures along the highway); Paul Aiello (Illinois Secretary of State); Mary Ann Atkins; Julia Lazicki; Robert Pruter (Lewis University Library); Theodore Cable (for sending news stories about I-55 and trips to the Loop); Melissa Cox (Lifeshots Photography); Shelly Cox (Missouri Department of Conservation); Tom Fitch, Linda Garvert and Curtis Mann (Sangamon Valley Collection, Lincoln Library); Tom Huber (Illinois State Library); William R. Iseminger (Cahokia Mounds State Historic Site); Tina Jordan and Judith Modelski (University of Michigan); Bill Kemp (McLean County Museum of History); Susan Krusemark (Illinois State Geological Survey); Keith Lynch (Kansas State University); Kate Murphy (Fleishman-Hillard, Willis Tower); Karen Perrin, Monica A. Prisco and Joseph Putnam (Illinois Department of Transportation); and Jessica Reese (Brookfield Zoo). Wayne Maley, coauthor with Ted of *Driving Across Kansas*, provided information and inspiration for some of the agriculture-related stories. We would also like to thank the landowners and business owners whom we interviewed along I-55 and whose names we list as interviewees at the end this book.

Acknowledgements

LuAnn would like to thank her husband, Mike, whom she met at mile 160 and married at mile 100, and her daughters, Rose and Lillian, for their artistic contributions and their hugs when she returned from the road. Ted would like to thank his wife, Diane, for her encouragement and support.

INTRODUCTION

Welcome to Illinois! Illinois is not only the "Land of Lincoln" (as the license plates on passing cars will constantly remind you) but also the land of bountiful harvests, slow-moving rivers and prairie sunsets. It is teeming with coal and corn, trains and trucks, beans and big cities. This book will connect you to all of these things, giving you a refreshingly new perspective on the familiar landscape along Interstate 55. While other highway travelers pass their time counting cornfields, you'll be watching for a spaceship near mile 36, shuddering from stories of the human-devouring piasa bird near mile 39, looking at a Hollywood movie set at mile 234 and learning about Illinois history, natural history, people and places that you'll be passing each mile of the way.

The route between Chicago and St. Louis was well traveled long before the paved lanes of Interstate 55 crossed the prairie. Our book will entwine your journey with those who traveled along this way centuries before you, as well as with those who live and work along this route today.

Remnants of a prehistoric path used by people and animals mark the first "highway" between southern and northern Illinois. Later, Native Americans, missionaries and pioneers used this trail. In 1812, the trail was named Edwards Trace after Ninian Edwards and the nearly four hundred soldiers who marched north to protect Peoria's Fort Clark during the War of 1812. Between Edwardsville and Elkhart, you'll travel alongside part of the Edwards Trace. During Edwards's march north, troops had neither mile markers nor towns to chart their way. Somewhere beyond your lane lines,

Introduction

you'll pass their early nineteenth-century natural history markers of Dry Point, Honey Point, Slab Point, Lake Fork, Brush Creek and Sugar Creek.

An 1882 history of Madison County records that the first mile markers on the southern half of our I-55 route appeared as early as 1820. The work noted that "county authorities laid out and opened a road from Edwardsville to Clear Lake on the Sangamon, a distance of seventy miles, as early as 1820, surveyed by Jacob Judy, who caused mile posts to be erected along the entire length of the said road, which is known to our readers as the 'Springfield' road."

By the mid-1860s, the railroad had become the "highway" between St. Louis and Chicago. As you roll alongside the rails of the former Chicago & Alton Railroad, we'll tell you stories of the immigrants who lost their lives laying the tracks, the celebrations that welcomed the new transportation route, the wealthy businessmen who built their mansions prominently near the tracks, the towns that sprouted along the line and the mourners who stood stoically along the tracks, honoring the final return of their beloved sixteenth president of the United States.

For those who preferred to travel the dusty road from south to north, the path became more trodden over the years. The August 1915 issue of *Illinois Highways* proclaimed the road to Chicago as the "Pontiac Trail." Complete with mile markers and road signs illustrated with an Indian holding a map of Illinois, the Pontiac Trail caught the publication's attention: "This trail will inevitably become the great thoroughfare of the State, connecting as it does, its largest city with the metropolis of its western border, and passing through its capital as well as many other prosperous cities and villages, and the heart of the corn belt."

While the writers of *Illinois Highways* foretold the immense importance of this route through the state, they had no idea that it would eventually become part of the country's most cherished national thoroughfare in a little over a decade. A few years after the Pontiac Trail, the road became designated as State Bond Issue 4 (SBI 4), and finally, in 1926, Route 66 was born. Over the decades, word spread worldwide of the legendary Route 66—the road trip highway through America that spanned 2,400 miles from Chicago to Los Angeles.

While our journey on I-55 crosses and parallels the beloved Route 66, our book is targeted on the less loved Interstate 55. Eisenhower's 1956 Federal Highway Aid act proposed a national network of highways and foretold the end of Route 66 and the beginning of Interstate 55. By the mid-1970s, I-55 had become the new major thoroughfare from Chicago to St. Louis. While

Introduction

Route 66 celebrates the past, our book will bring you up to speed with its modern-day equivalent. We will revel in some stories of the past and reveal new tales to celebrate in the present.

During your journey, you'll hear the stories of both the pioneers who found their home on the prairie between St. Louis and Chicago and today's hardworking farmers, business owners and landowners who eat their breakfast, do their daily tasks and sleep within sound of the hum of the interstate's evening transit.

The Honorable Joseph Gillespie sang the praises of the state's "genuine pioneers," as he described them, the "old Indian fighters" who settled here among the original Indian tribes of Illinois. On October 16, 1874, he gathered together the old settlers in Madison County to honor the early pioneers and record their stories for all generations to come: "There never was a class of men who combined the same degree of perfection, the qualities of hunter, farmer, soldier, and patriot, as did our Indian fighters… How few of us ever think of the perils and privations of those who preceded us in these wilds, much less to honor them as they deserve."

We'll share tales of "genuine pioneers" and their "perils and privations," as well as landowners who lived adjacent to the current lanes of I-55 like Robert Pulliam, Isaac Funk, William R. Duncan and Lewis Thomas.

As we take you through the Land of Lincoln, we'll share multiple accounts of Illinois' most famous president. We'll tell you of the humble little Sangamon River that he used as his highway into central Illinois; of his influence in Springfield, where he made his home with his family; of historic Elkhart, where he traveled his circuit as lawyer; of the town named for him before he died; and of the Abraham Lincoln National Cemetery near Joliet.

While our book gives readers a window to what the past looked like along this route, it also documents a history of this highway for future travelers. We'll record the stories of present landowners and business owners like Marilyn and Ed Banovic, Dave Hammond, Harold Carter and Diane Sullivan, all of whom make their living along this route, and of the farms, factories and businesses that are the heartbeat of the prairie outside your car window.

Prairies, moraines, wildflowers, birds, clouds, storms, wetlands and rivers are the elements of the greater setting beyond the lanes of I-55. We'll paint pictures of what the land looked like when the pioneers first encountered it and compare it to the natural history that you'll be seeing on your drive.

While we wrote our book with the intention of answering an oft-repeated question along the interstate—"What is that?"—we'll also answer a multitude

Introduction

of other questions along the interstate. We'll tell you about the electrical power flowing above your head and the oil flowing below. We'll describe the transportation chain that moves the crops in the fields to elevators, grain bins and factories, where they are made into products and stored in warehouses until they are shipped by truck, train or barge to your home. We'll reveal mysteries about the war to erect the tallest modern structure on the flat Springfield landscape, of an Illinois-shaped pond and of monstrous creatures reported along the I-55 route.

Whether you read this book in the quiet safety of your home or as a vehicle's passenger, narrating the trip for friends or family, we hope that you enjoy each mile across Illinois and can say by your journey's end, "There really *is* more than corn along this highway."

Part I
STATE SYMBOLS AND A HIGHWAY GUIDE

Illinois State Symbols

Look for these state symbols as you drive along Interstate 55.

Illinois State Flag

The state flag that you'll see flying at rest stops along I-55 is a version redesigned for recognition. The illustration on the flag is of the state seal. The seal is also redesigned from its original illustration in 1819. The bald eagle represents the national bird of the United States. The banner in its beak is the state motto. The shield displays thirteen stars and stripes for the original colonies. The rock has the year Illinois entered statehood and the year the state seal was redesigned. The ground and sun represent the bounty of the fertile Illinois prairie.

 Today's flag looks almost identical to the original that was designed in 1915 except for the addition of one very important word. While serving in Vietnam, Chief Petty Officer Bruce McDaniel of Waverly could see a bit of home in his state flag on the mess hall wall each day. However, too many times, he heard soldiers wonder whose state it represented. McDaniel returned home and asked that the state's name be placed on the flag so all would be able to identify the flag of Illinois. In 1970, the word "Illinois" was added to the state flag.

Traveling through Illinois

Illinois state flag. *LuAnn Cadden.*

Today's seal looks almost identical to its previous 1839 illustration except for a controversial change to the banner. If you look carefully at the banner in the eagle's beak, you'll notice that the word "sovereignty" is upside down. This wasn't always so. In 1867, Secretary of State Sharon Tyndale suggested that the state seal be updated. In response to the Civil War, he believed, "National Union" should come before "State Sovereignty." The state Senate did not approve of that change but did approve of other minor changes. When Tyndale turned in the final draft, he kept the order of "State Sovereignty, National Union" but flipped the word "sovereignty" so that "National Union" would stand out more prominently...and more legibly.

State Bird: Northern Cardinal

The northern cardinal is the state bird of seven U.S. states. It has been the Illinois state bird since 1929. Cardinals live in all of the states east of the Rocky Mountains and south into most of Central America. Their striking red feathers and identifiable head crest make them one of the most easily recognized birds in the country.

STATE SYMBOLS AND A HIGHWAY GUIDE

Northern Cardinal. *Shelly Cox.*

Many people refer to cardinals as "redbirds." And when referring to them with this nickname, they are most often talking about the colorful male bird, whose bright red plumage attracts the neighboring females. With her beautiful mixture of olive, brown and red feathers, she will remain better camouflaged in the shrubby areas where they build their nests. At mile 161N in Bloomington-Normal, you can see Reggie Redbird, the Illinois State University mascot, painted prominently on a water tower. In some illustrations, Reggie is made to look fierce and intimidating to his opponents as he snarls with a beak full of teeth. The cardinals we see at our feeders don't need teeth to crack open sunflower seeds in one easy snap. Their deep orange triangular bill is powerful enough.

Cardinals are the most popular birds to grace the covers of Christmas cards, and it is no wonder. Nothing can portray the contrast of warmth and cold so well as the lively red flittering of a cardinal's bright wings to a still blanket of white snow. In winter, they often flock together at feeders and brighten leafless snow-covered branches. Sometimes their colorful stillness glows like bulbs that give life to a Christmas tree, while at other times, their wings, flashing as they flutter from higher branches to the ground, fall like confetti in celebration of the New Year.

Traveling through Illinois

State Flower: Blue Violet

One of the most common flowers to find along U.S. interstate highways is the little violet, barely noticed as it stays low to the ground, hidden in the grass after its spring flowers have fallen off its delicate stems. In 1907, this European native became the state flower of Illinois.

Although there are yellow and white violets, the people of Illinois chose the common blue violet as their preferred hue. In the language of flowers, violets most often represent humility or modesty. Their heart-shaped leaves may also lend them to stories of love. One of those stories is a Greek legend about the beautiful nymph Io, much loved by Zeus. In order to protect Io from Hera, his jealous queen, he changed Io into a white heifer so that she could live safely in the fields. The coarse grass brought Io to tears, and so Zeus transformed her tears into the tender violet to soften the ground she walked on and to sweeten the food she ate.

Violets are hardy and tolerant. Because they are so prolific, many people consider them a weed in their lawns, gardens and fields. Other generations

Blue violet. *LuAnn Cadden.*

used to prize them for their many medicinal properties, from calming headaches to easing skin cancers.

As you drive by at sixty-five miles per hour, you surely will not be able to see the humble violet blending in with the grass along the road or in the fields, but it is there. So, when you stretch your legs at a rest stop or pull off to get some food or fuel, scan the lawn under your feet or the grass along the sidewalk, and you might just see our modest yet mighty state flower.

State Insect: Monarch Butterfly

In 1974, a third-grade class in Decatur suggested that the monarch butterfly should be the state insect of Illinois. And why not? This butterfly definitely deserves its royal status as king. While this orange and black butterfly feeds on the nectar of various wildflowers, it lays its eggs only on milkweed plants—the sole food its tiny yellow-, black- and white-striped caterpillars depend on. Without prairie refueling spots in gardens and along the roadsides, the monarchs wouldn't be able to successfully make their annual three-thousand-mile fall migration from Canada to Mexico. Most

Monarch butterfly. *Shelly Cox.*

butterfly species don't live for more than two months, but monarchs have a "super-generation" that fly to Mexico, overwinter in the fir-covered hillsides of the Transvolcanic Mountains, fly back through the United States—where they lay their eggs on milkweed plants—and then finally die after nine long months.

In late summer, black and orange wings fill the skies across the eastern United States and funnel south into a migration path over Texas toward Mexico. In mid- to late September, those monarchs are usually passing heavily through Illinois, and if you look carefully, you'll notice them flutter past your window every so often. You may see them among the roadside prairie plants and milkweed near mile 127N or 142S. You might also see them up close near the rest stop stream at mile 195S or in the rest stop flower bed at mile 27N.

State Prairie Grass: Big Bluestem

Big bluestem. *Ted Cable.*

The land that became the state of Illinois was covered by prairie grasses. Big bluestem may have been the most widespread and abundant grass throughout the true prairie. It grows in such tall and dense stands that it often prevents other grasses from growing around it by shading them out. In the past, this resulted in large areas of almost pure big bluestem in the prairies.

Big bluestem grows to a height of ten feet. It has tall, slender stems. The grass is green throughout much of the summer; the stem turns blue-purple as it matures, hence the name. The seed heads usually have three spiky projections and resemble a turkey foot. Big bluestem has deep roots and strong rhizomes. Consequently, it forms very strong sod and serves as excellent forage. It also yields two to four tons of hay per acre.

State Symbols and a Highway Guide

State Soil: Drummer Silty Clay Loam

A state bird, a state tree and a state flower are common state symbols that first come to mind when naming state symbols, but a state soil? Actually, in this state, whose nickname is the Prairie State, a state soil, announced in 2001, seems very fitting. The deep roots of thick prairie grasses and wildflowers aid the richness of this soil. After drummer soil formed twenty-five thousand years ago from glaciers that left behind forty- to sixty-inch layers of a powdery wind-blown (loess) soil, prairie plants took root and tunneled down sixteen feet deep. As the roots died and decomposed, they created deep, dark, brown, nutrient-rich topsoil. Below this gardener's dream soil is a two-foot-thick subsoil layer that has some moist clay, and below that layer is mostly loam, a layer where plant roots thrive.

Nearly 1.5 million acres of land in Illinois is drummer silty clay loam. As you pass miles 142S, 40N and 127N, you'll see the native wildflowers and grasses at work, creating more rich soil with their network of roots. For most of the miles along your journey, you can appreciate the harvest of soybeans, corn and wheat that benefit from this fertile soil and that make Illinois the breadbasket for the rest of the country. In "A New Eden: The Pioneer Era in Sangamon County" in the 1974 book *Illinois: A History of the Prairie State*, Robert P. Howard wrote:

> *In mid-state the first farmers were just beginning to realize that it is not true that where the oaks grew tallest the soil was richest. In their grandchildren's generation, soil scientists would explain why the best soil was on the prairie, where the fibrous roots of the wild bluestem grass for centuries had produced humus of great natural fertility... The upland timber soil had only 25 to 50 per cent as much organic matter as the brown silt loams of the more undulating prairies or the black gumbo of the flatlands.*

State Tree: White Oak

In 1907, schoolchildren voted that the native oak should be the state tree. But there are many varieties of oak in Illinois, and seventy years later, the grandchildren of those schoolchildren chose a more specific oak that would represent the arbor of the state. In 1973, the state tree changed to the white oak, a tree that is found in every county of the state.

Traveling through Illinois

White oak. *Keith Lynch.*

"Mighty oaks from little acorns grow" into strong neighbors that can witness the comings and goings of homes and families for nearly four centuries. The wide, thick branches—which can rise up to one hundred feet along their whitish-gray trunk—have provided the perfect climbing limbs for generations of children. The thick, dark leaves make a great sheltering tree for a home or a shady spot to enjoy a good book. The greenish-brown acorns provide food for squirrels, turkey, deer, songbirds and other animals. While the strong wood provided tools, fences and homes for early settlers, we see it today in the furniture and flooring in many homes.

Most of the drive along I-55 is devoid of trees, but you will notice some deliberate woody rows between crop fields, others sheltering homesteads and barns and a few other survivors standing quite alone in huge fields. The rest stops along the highway also provide shady retreats under varied canopies that will include some oak trees.

Sometimes, the huge, sprawling oaks in the fields are bur oak trees. In *Reading the Landscape of America*, May Theilgaard Watts noted, "We felt the thick bark and corky twigs of the old bur oaks, and understood how this oak, rather than the red oak, or the white oak, could have withstood the Indian fires that swept the prairies and licked at the margin of the forest." At mile 45N, you will travel through one of the most forested areas of this highway and get to admire some of Illinois' oaks. You will also see them up close at multiple rest areas.

State Fossil: Tully Monster

The "Tully monster" lived along the edge of the shallow tropical waters that existed here during the Pennsylvanian geologic period (Coal Age). It was a soft-bodied, predatory creature less than ten inches long, and it was found only in this part of the country. In 1989, it was designated the state fossil of Illinois.

Although it was not really a "monster," it got its name from its bizarre appearance and body shape. The Tully monster had a pair of triangular-shaped fins at the tail, a dorsal fin and a long snout with a claw-like structure at the end and eight small, sharp teeth. A stalk protruded from both sides of the body, forming a crossbar, with an eye or other sensory organ at its tip.

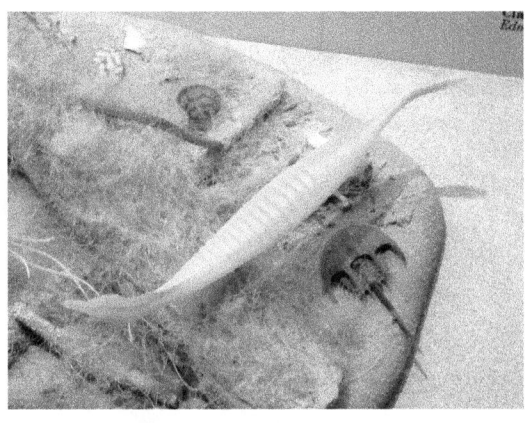

The slender Tully monster surrounded by other sea creatures. *LuAnn Cadden.*

At mile 213, you will cross over the little Mazon River, where amateur fossil collector Francis Tully first found the Tully monster fossil in 1958.

Guiding You Along the Highway

The bulk of our book is divided into two large parts: the route southbound from Chicago to St. Louis and the route northbound from St. Louis to Chicago. However, the stories going northbound are mostly different than the stories going southbound. While some stories repeat because landmarks can be seen equally well from either direction, new stories are included for landmarks only seen well from one direction.

We mark each of our roadway stories with the mile markers that lead you down the highway. When choosing the subjects at each mile marker, we prioritized potential stories using the following criteria:

- first choice: the reader can see the landmark
- second choice: the reader can see a road sign that relates to the story
- third choice: the natural history of that location is prominent

For your driving safety, we do not list stories to mile markers within the city limits of Chicago. Rather than having you try to scan the sides of the road searching for signs, usually hidden by traffic, we tell the stories of the neighborhoods through which you are passing.

Part II
SOUTHBOUND

CHICAGO

What do you think of when you hear the word "Chicago"? Do you think of Judy Garland's "tottlin' town" and "State Street, that Great Street"? Maybe you agree with Frank Sinatra as he croons, "My Kind of Town (Chicago Is)." Or, like the Blues Brothers, maybe you feel a nostalgic hometown connection to "Sweet Home Chicago." It is no wonder that these and more than three hundred other songs have been written to celebrate this beautiful city on the lake. If you've shopped along the Michigan Mile, strolled through the Art Institute, had cocktails at the top of the Hancock or high tea at the Drake, watched baseball behind the ivy wall or on the South Side or taken sunset cruises on the Chicago River that reveal the grandeur of the city lights, you know that Chicago has many stories to tell.

Chicago's first permanent resident was a trader named Jean Baptiste Point du Sable, who set up an outpost here in the late 1770s. He had been born in Haiti to a French father and African slave mother and came here via New Orleans. In 1795, the government built Fort Dearborn where the Chicago River met the shoreline of Lake Michigan at what now is the Michigan Avenue Bridge, thereby encouraging settlement on what was then the western frontier. In 1812, Indians burned the fort to the ground. The fort was rebuilt, but this would not be the last time that people here would rebuild from ashes.

Nearly sixty years later, fire again destroyed Chicago. Tens of thousands of buildings spread over 2,600 acres burned, and between two hundred and three hundred people died in the Great Chicago Fire of 1871. The fire was particularly destructive because virtually all of the buildings and even sidewalks were made of wood. Although the fire did apparently start in Catherine O'Leary's barn, the story of the cow kicking over the lantern is a myth propagated by a newspaper reporter. Mrs. O'Leary, who died in 1895, spent the rest of her life feeling responsible for the fire.

The widespread devastation provided a unique opportunity for world-renowned architects, such as Louis Sullivan, to build a city from scratch. Like a phoenix, Chicago rose from the ashes larger and more uniquely American than any other U.S. city. The first steel-framed skyscrapers are considered to be architectural masterpieces. The debris from the fire was dumped into the lake to create fill for parks along the Lake Michigan shoreline (which at the time was near present-day Michigan Avenue), creating land for what is now the Museum Campus, Grant Park and Millennium Park.

Although it is often blustery along the lakefront and in the Loop's skyscraper canyons, the "Windy City" nickname has nothing to do with the breezes. It was coined in 1893 by the *New York Sun* newspaper editor when commenting on the blustery and boastful Chicago politicians. While Chicago and New York competed to host the 1893 World's Fair, *New York Sun* editor Charles Dana warned not to listen "to the nonsensical claims of that windy city. Its people could not build a World's Fair even if they won it." In spite of the atmospheric and political winds, Chicago did win the competition and created a wildly successful World's Fair celebrating the 400th anniversary of Columbus's arrival in the New World.

Mark Twain wrote, "It is hopeless for the occasional visitor to try to keep up with Chicago. She outgrows his prophecies faster than he can make them." That puts us in a precarious position of attempting to prophesize what you might see as you drive through the southwest part of the city on your way out of town. However, we do know that you will be traveling through diverse working-class neighborhoods. In 1916, Carl Sandburg described Chicago as:

> *Hog butcher for the world,*
> *Tool maker, stacker of wheat,*
> *Player with railroads and the nation's freight handler;*
> *Stormy, husky, brawling,*
> *City of the big shoulders.*

He added that Chicagoans are *proud* to be these things. The neighborhoods that you'll be passing through grew around Sandburg's stockyards and railroads, factories and freight. Today, they are still stormy, husky and brawling but also vibrant and colorful enclaves of proud working-class people.

Chicago is a multicultural city. If you exit I-55, you may enter a neighborhood that is a little piece of Mexico, Italy, Ireland, Poland, Puerto Rico or China. Rather than a melting pot, Chicago is more like a colorful quilt consisting of seventy-seven distinct neighborhoods, including Greek Town, Little Italy, Little Seoul, Chinatown, Swedish Andersonville and several Hispanic, Lithuanian and Polish neighborhoods. You can take a veritable trip around the world as you slice through this urban cross section of cultural diversity.

Leaving the Lakefront

After merging onto I-55, the Bronzeville (293) neighborhood will be on your left. It has been home to African Americans since the "Great Migration" brought them here from the South for jobs in the twentieth century. Many jazz and blues musicians called Bronzeville home, including Louis Armstrong, Muddy Waters, Buddy Guy, Willie Dixon and Lou Rawls.

At the busy I-94 and I-90 junction, you'll pass Chinatown on your left. Chicago's Chinatown is the fourth largest in the United States, with fifteen thousand Chinese residents and scores of Chinese restaurants and other businesses.

As you head southwest, you'll pass neighborhoods such as Bridgeport, famous for producing five mayors, including Richard M. Daley and his father, Richard J. Daley. For most of its history, Irish and eastern European families lived here; their lives centered on beautiful and vital churches, the steeples of which you can see in the distance as you drive along. Many early Irish residents worked on the Erie Canal and moved here to help dig the Illinois & Michigan (I&M) Canal, which you will see later in your journey. In fact, you'll be driving along the route walked by Native Americans and explorers when portaging between the Chicago River and Des Plaines River prior to canal construction.

You also will pass through what has been called the Bungalow Belt, referring to the famous Chicago bungalow style of homes built in the 1950s. These neighborhoods are a mixture of Polish and Mexican cultures, making them a place where "Witamy meets Bienvenidos" as visitors are welcomed in both Polish and Spanish. Indicative of this cultural mix and the dynamic, ever-changing nature of these neighborhoods, the Pilsen neighborhood, which Czech immigrants named after the city in the Czech Republic, is now an enclave of Mexican Americans.

Western Avenue (290) marks what was once Chicago's western boundary. It is 24.5 miles long, making it Chicago's longest continuous street and one of the longest urban streets in the world. Pulaski Road (287) is another sign of the Polish influence in these neighborhoods. On the first Monday of every March, Chicago celebrates Casimir Pulaski Day, and schools and government offices close in honor of this military leader from Poland who became an American Revolutionary War general.

As you are heading out of Chicago, I-55 is surrounded by railroad lines and waterways, as well as airplanes flying above. Chicago was ideally situated to become a transportation and commerce center. In 1848, the Illinois & Michigan Canal (250) linked the Great Lakes with the Mississippi River. East–west rail lines and later highways curved around the south end of Lake Michigan, creating a constricted and concentrated transportation corridor through the Chicago area. Today, half of the nation's railroad freight passes through Chicago. The combined air

Canal Street Bridge, 1899. River traffic necessitated the building of the Chicago Sanitary & Ship Canal. *Howard and Lois Adelmann Regional History Collection at Lewis University.*

Southbound

traffic at Midway and O'Hare Airports makes Chicago the busiest aviation center. You'll pass the exit to nearby Midway Airport at Cicero Avenue (286) and will see much of this air and rail traffic as you drive along the Stevenson Expressway.

After Harlem Avenue, near mile 282, you'll quickly cross over the Chicago Sanitary and Ship Canal, which replaced the I&M Canal in 1900. The same water churned up by downtown Chicago River sightseeing boats flows through the canal into the Des Plaines River, which you'll cross near mile 279 and again at 247. The canal empties Chicago of its treated sewage and supports commerce-driven barge traffic. It's the aquatic counterpart of the interstate's semi-trailer congestion. That Chicago's sewage is flowing south through the canal is the result of what is considered one of the Seven Engineering Wonders of the World. The Chicago River, and hence the sewage that was put into it, originally flowed into Lake Michigan, the source of Chicago's drinking water. Engineers reversed the flow of the Chicago River with a series of locks, much to the outrage of Peoria, St. Louis and other downstream cities.

From Chicago to St. Louis

Near mile 278, you'll exit Cook County near the busy intersection of I-294 and I-55. As you travel farther out into the suburbs, we will begin to use mile markers to place our stories. We hope that you drive safely while you enjoy these stories.

277: DuPage County

Almost 1 million people live in DuPage County, making it second only to Cook as Illinois' most populous county. It was named after the river that flows through it, which in turn was named after a French fur trapper. Today, DuPage County furs are in closets as it is the wealthiest county in Illinois, and its per capita income is among the highest in the nation.

275: Suburban Signals

Water towers rising above the flat urban landscape signal that you have entered the suburbs. The towers on the right supply water to Willowbrook.

Such towers, proudly labeled with the names of their communities, often provide the only indication that you have crossed from one suburb into another. These community landmarks stand in the nondescript suburban landscape like lofty road signs. A typical water tower holds about 100,000 gallons of water—that's about the amount of water in fifty backyard in-ground swimming pools. These tall towers hold excess water for the community and provide consistent pressure to keep water flowing. If you have a water tower in your town, your fire insurance rates may be lower than in towns without towers because the tower assures adequate pressure for fire hydrants. You'll see water towers throughout your drive along I-55, and ahead you will see artistic ones, like the one at mile 161 with Illinois State University's Reggie Redbird painted on the side and the one for Atlanta at mile 139 with a bright yellow smiley face beaming over the community.

271: Lithuanian Center

Even here on the city's edge you'll find patches of the colorful ethnic quilt that is Chicagoland. Exit 271 takes you to the Lithuanian World Center, a showcase of the Lithuanian culture that permeates this area. More than 100,000 Lithuanian immigrants live in the Chicago Metropolitan Area, making this the greatest concentration of Lithuanians in the United States. Half of that population immigrated here between 1880 and 1914, fleeing from Russian oppression and becoming the integral sweat and muscle that kept Chicago's factories productive. By 1923, the population had reached 90,000 people. Two more waves of immigration occurred after Soviet Union occupation in World War II and after Lithuania's independence in 1991.

The 120,000-square-foot Lithuanian World Center was built in 1988. While it inspires Lithuanians to celebrate their native culture in dance, folk music and art, it is a community resource center to all ethnicities. The center enrolls hundreds of students in classes on Lithuanian culture and language. This is one of two major Lithuanian cultural centers in Chicago. The other is the Balzekas Museum of Lithuanian Culture, off Pulaski Road back at mile 288. Both institutions inspire young Lithuanians and remind all of us of the influence that Lithuanians had on building Chicago.

Southbound

268: A Taste of Route 66

Back at mile 271, a brown "Historic Route 66" sign harkens back to early road trips through this iconic corridor. You'll see many more of these signs along your drive toward St. Louis. Even though I-55 now dominates the path south, some establishments from Route 66's heyday survived to give us a taste of the past. For almost a century, travelers coming to and from Chicago have dined at the White Fence Farm, exit 268, that boasts the "World's Best Chicken," with chickens shipped in daily and coated with a secret breading milled in Chicago.

If only there could be a sensory-rich "Route 66 Restaurant Museum" where you could breathe in the flavorful smells of the old road favorites, bottled and preserved for history; gather favorite recipes; hear the distinct chatter and clang of each restaurant; and, ultimately, even taste a few dishes that have slipped into Route 66 history—like the ham sandwiches with Ernie's special sauce served at the now-closed Pig Hip Restaurant in Broadwell (mile 119). Luckily, some classic eateries, like White Fence, still exist along your I-55 route. Ahead you can still stop for a fried bologna or grilled SPAM sandwich at the Palms Grill Café in Atlanta, established in 1934. In Springfield, you can bite into a crisp corn dog at the Cozy Drive-In, where corn dogs were invented and have been served since 1949. Or you can savor the home-style meals and family-inspired baklava still served at the Ariston Café, established in Litchfield in 1924. With pride, many communities along I-55 have preserved Route 66 history, oftentimes in the form of food. Perhaps you'll share in this taste of history today.

265: Wherefore Art Thou Romeoville?

The next two exits lead to Romeoville. Romeoville was named after the Shakespearean hero and was planned as a twin city to compete with nearby Juliet. Romeoville traces its history to the I&M Canal (mile 250). Land on each side of the canal was divided into town lots and sold. The town of Lockport was laid out at one of the canal locks. One town (Romeo) was laid out four miles north of the lock, and another town (Juliet) was founded four miles south of the lock. Years later, after Juliet's name was changed to honor the famous explorer Louis Joliet, Romeo's name was changed to Romeoville. Romeoville was nicknamed "Stone City" because of its stone quarries, one of which produced the stone for the Illinois capitol. Romeoville is noteworthy for the Romeoville Prairie, home of the Hines emerald green dragonfly, a rare and endangered insect. Romeoville also is home to the McDonald's research and innovation facility that develops designs for its restaurants worldwide.

262: Dale Coyne Racing

Hopefully, you're obeying the speed limit today and not racing like an Indy car down the highway. Leave that to the professionals of the Dale Coyne Racing team, whose headquarters is ahead on your left. At night, from I-55, you can see the spotlighted retired race car that glows in the lobby. Dale Coyne is a retired race car driver who started his own team of professional Indy car racers in the mid-1980s. In 1994, he gained a co-owner with Chicago Bears Hall of Famer and racing enthusiast Walter Payton. His drivers have come from more than a dozen countries. Indy cars are "open wheel" and "open cockpit" cars, which means that the wheels are positioned outside the car's body, and there is no roof over the driver's head. These cars can speed in excess of 230 miles per hour on large tracks, such as the famed one in Indianapolis. On the straight track of I-55, you travel less than one-third of that speed.

261: Mighty Phragmites

The stand of tall grass along the roadside here and ahead at mile 256 is *Phragmites*, or common reed. To call it "common" is to understate its abundance. *Phragmites* is found in every state and on every continent. A particularly aggressive form of *Phragmites* spread into North America from Europe, probably arriving in East Coast ports, and has spread westward across the United States. It thrives in roadside ditches and other wet areas, often growing to a height of fifteen feet. In Illinois and throughout much of the nation, dense stands of this alien invader are choking out and replacing native vegetation in wetlands, making them less valuable for ducks and other wildlife and blocking views and access for recreation. Wetland managers try to control this destructive plant by using chemicals and fire and by disking up the stands, but these methods are expensive and have only temporary effectiveness. Researchers are trying to find better ways of controlling the *Phragmites* invasion.

The feathery plumes of invasive *Phragmites* in the fall. *Ted Cable.*

259: The Lincoln Highway

Ahead at exit 257, you will cross US 30, better known as the Lincoln Highway. Lincoln Highway was the first road to go from coast to coast, originally starting in Times Square in New York City and ending 3,389 miles later in Lincoln Park in San Francisco. It was the first national memorial to Abraham Lincoln. At 256N, read more about how the idea for this coast-to-coast route surfaced at a dinner party in 1912.

257: Sound Walls

These tan-colored walls protect neighborhoods from highway noise. Since 1976, people have had a legal right to a neighborhood free from highway traffic noise. The threshold for requiring noise reduction is sixty-seven decibels; noise levels above this impair a conversation between two people standing three feet apart. The effectiveness of sound walls depends on the distance between the listener and the wall. People living close to the wall experience increased privacy, cleaner air and healthier lawns and shrubs. They sleep more soundly, enjoy their yards more and even experience less stress.

However, these benefits quickly diminish as you move farther away from the wall. Some people doubt whether such walls are a sound investment, so to speak. They cost between $1.5 million and $4 million per mile to build, and they are not effective if openings exist for crossroads or utilities. Moreover, these walls do not prevent noise from reaching homes on hillsides or buildings rising above the wall. So these expensive walls may end up helping only a small number of nearby residents.

Many folks think that sound walls are ugly. You might wonder why trees are not used to reduce the noise. Trees would provide an aesthetically pleasing visual shield, but they are not nearly as effective at reducing noise levels as a solid barrier. It would take at least one hundred feet of dense vegetation to provide the same acoustical benefit as the smallest feasible noise wall, and it would require a strip of trees two hundred feet wide to reduce noise by ten decibels. Obviously, it is not feasible to plant enough vegetation along urban highways to achieve such noise reductions. In the future, quieter vehicles may make these walls unnecessary.

254: From Forlorn Lover to French Explorer

Stories abound about the naming of the town of Joliet. It may have been named as Juliet to complement the nearby town of Romeo. It might have been named for one of the founder's relatives or for Mount Joliet or to honor the French explorer who traveled through here in 1673 with Jacques Marquette. A 1674 map identifies a ridge along the Des Plaines River as Mont Joliet. A 1778 map calls this area Juliet. The similarly named geographical feature and town confused mapmakers. Supposedly, in 1845, President Martin Van Buren put an end to the confusion, and the town of Juliet became Joliet. While Juliet dreamed upon the stars about her Romeo and Louis Joliet used them for navigation, starry nights may have inspired Joliet native John Houbolt to design the first Lunar Module. At 248N, read how the first soft-serve ice cream cones started a royal dairy business in Joliet.

SOUTHBOUND

252: Coast-to-Coast Highways

At exit 257, you crossed US 30, the first coast-to-coast highway, which stretched from New York City to San Francisco. Just ahead, at mile 250, you will be crossing Interstate 80, another such highway. Although built in different eras, both of these roads parallel each other and even become the same highway in stretches as they cross North America. Interstate 80 is the second-longest highway in the United States (I-90 from Seattle to Boston is the first), stretching more than 2,900 miles from the outskirts of New York City to San Francisco. From here, heading west to San Francisco, it connects Omaha, Salt Lake City, Reno and Sacramento. To the east, it provides the most direct route to Cleveland and New York City. For much of the way across Nebraska and Wyoming, I-80 follows the route of an important nineteenth-century cross-country highway: the Oregon Trail.

251: From New Zealand Farmers to You

The fifty-thousand-square-foot Fronterra warehouse on the right, like others you have seen in the past few miles, stores and distributes food items. Fronterra is the world's leading exporter of dairy products and ships products from New Zealand to 140 countries. Fronterra is cooperatively owned by eleven thousand New Zealand dairy farmers, and like most other firms along this stretch of highway, Fronterra chose this location because Chicago is considered to be a central point for U.S. product distribution. Dairy products arrive from New Zealand to U.S. seaports and are then sent here by rail. Up to twenty trucks per day then move the products from this warehouse to customers. Before leasing the warehouse to Fronterra, the owner installed a security fence to meet conditions of the Partnership Against Terrorism Act that requires cargo handling areas for imported products to be protected.

250: I&M Canal

Ahead, you will cross the historic Illinois & Michigan Canal, another coast-to-coast transportation corridor. Construction of the canal brought laborers (to dig the canal by hand) and land speculators from around the world. In 1848, this canal opened, completing the long anticipated continuous water

Traveling through Illinois

Mules hauling a canalboat. *Howard and Lois Adelmann Regional History Collection at Lewis University.*

route from the Atlantic Ocean to the Gulf of Mexico. It stretched ninety-seven miles and was six feet deep and sixty feet across at the top.

The I&M Canal brought streams of people and commerce to Chicago from the East and the South. People from the East could take the Erie Canal to Buffalo, New York, and then steamboats to Chicago via the Great Lakes. At Chicago, travelers would board canalboats. Mules or horses walking along adjacent towpaths pulled the boats at five to six miles per hour to the Illinois River at La Salle. Riverboats carried passengers down the Illinois to the Mississippi River and on to St. Louis or New Orleans. Many folks who traveled the famous western wagon trails, like the Oregon Trail, first traveled the I&M Canal. In the early 1900s, traffic on the canal stopped as freight shipments moved to railroads and the Chicago Sanitary and Ship Canal, which you crossed over near mile 282.

In 1984, President Reagan signed legislation establishing this as the nation's *first* National Heritage Corridor. Today, the canal is a transportation corridor for hikers, bikers and canoeists, with historic sites scattered along the way. You can even take a cruise on a replica canalboat, complete with costumed guides, so you can relive the experience of traveling on the canal that shaped the history of the Midwest. Ahead, you'll cross over the Des Plaines River. Now connected to the Chicago Sanitary and Ship Canal, it carries the commercial river traffic.

Southbound

247: Refining a Healthier Oil

Along this stretch of highway, you will see oil refineries, like ExxonMobil (244N) ahead on your left, producing petroleum products. Down the road you will see croplands producing soy oil. But ahead, on the right, just after crossing the Des Plaines River, you can see the entrance and buildings of the IOI Group's Loders Croklaan oil processing factory, which refines palm tree oil for use in baking and processed foods. For more than one hundred years, Loders Croklaan has been a leading producer of oils and fats for the food industry. Palm oil, rich in nutrients and a healthier alternative to partially hydrogenated fats, is becoming even more important as the government and food manufacturers focus on reducing trans fat from our foods. The IOI Group has more than ten thousand employees, mostly working on its 370,000 acres of palm plantations in Malaysia. The oil from those Malaysian palm plantations is processed here and ultimately finds its ways into many of our foods, including bakery goods, margarines and peanut butters.

245: War and Peace

Arsenal Road (exit 245) is named for the Joliet Army Ammunition Plant formerly called the Joliet Arsenal, where the U.S. Army made more than 4 billion pounds of explosives. During World War II it was considered the largest and most advanced ammunition plant in the world, employing more than ten thousand people and making more than 926 million bombs, shells, mines, detonators, and fuses, as well as more than 1 billion pounds of TNT!

Read more at 245N about this site, which was transformed into the beautiful Midewin National Tallgrass Prairie and the peaceful Abraham Lincoln National Cemetery.

243: Urban Wilderness

On the right is a sportsman's paradise and nature lover's retreat. The 5,400-acre Des Plaines Wildlife and Conservation Area provides an abundance of fish and wildlife, camping and picnic areas, hiking and equestrian trails and shooting sports ranges. The area includes 200 acres of water and boating access to the Kankakee River. Pheasant hunting is the most popular type of hunting here, although some hunters pursue deer, coyote, rabbits and doves.

About 80 acres are set aside as a nature preserve to protect and manage a natural prairie area. From your car, in late summer, you may be able to see the tall sunflower-like tops of compass plant and the slender purple rods of blazing star. Throughout your drive toward St. Louis, you'll enjoy more prairie flowers in the medians and along the roadside, a remnant and reminder of this Prairie State's original landscape.

241: Kankakee River

At this mile, you will cross the Kankakee River. Kankakee is Mohegan for "wolf" or "wolf land," harkening back to the time when wolves roamed the Illinois prairies. The Kankakee is a ninety-mile-long tributary of the Illinois River with its headwaters in northern Indiana. It joins the Des Plaines River to form the Illinois River just west of here. Native Americans from many tribes traveled this river, as did French explorers and fur trappers. Since the late 1800s, the river has provided a weekend escape from the hectic, stressful city life of folks living in Chicago and the surrounding suburbs. It provides excellent fishing for smallmouth bass, northern pike and walleye.

237: Coal Cities

While arteries of water transported people and products above ground, black veins of coal beneath the soil pumped life into towns throughout Illinois. The 1820 discovery of coal gave birth to Coal City (exit 236) and the neighboring town of Diamond. Coal veins continuously changed the state map as towns appeared and then disappeared. When miners extracted the last bit of coal, the miners and their families moved on to the next mining town. Coal fueled commerce throughout the nineteenth and early twentieth centuries, just as gasoline and diesel does today. Steamships and steam engines that transferred goods across the country depended on coal miners to keep up with their demand for fuel.

Mining was dirty, dark and dangerous work for the men who labored hundreds of feet below the surface. Women feared the sound of the mournful whistle that announced that a mine had exploded, collapsed, flooded or caught fire. One mile west of exit 236, in Diamond, the state had one of its earliest mining accidents, described by a postcard written years later by George Atkins: "Diamond Mine Braidwood, Ill.—Mine flooded Feb 16,

1883 drowning 72 coal miners, including my father, Samuel Atkins, and his brother, John Atkins. I stood with Mother at the mouth of mine and watched the water boil up to the surface sealing doom of all below."

It took more than a month to pump the water out from the mine and to bring the first victims back above ground one last time before they were buried once again in their final resting place. Because of debris, the 46 other men were unable to be reached and were sealed inside the mine forever. The nation's third-worst mining disaster occurred just sixty miles west of here. Along the same ill-fated parallel as the Diamond Mine, the Cherry Mine caught fire and killed 259 men in 1909.

Coal was sometimes called "black diamond" because of its luster in sunlight. But these tragedies muted the "luster" of the coal from these mines. The 1909 disaster brought awareness for better safety procedures, spurred the first workers' compensation program in the United States and prompted the U.S. Bureau of Mines to establish more government oversight. Read more about labor unions at 46S.

From tragedy to renewal in Diamond. *Ted Cable.*

Today, coal is mined in fourteen Illinois counties, including several along I-55. In 2012, the twenty-four active mines produced more than 45 million tons of coal—the highest amount in twenty years. Illinois has the largest bituminous coal resources, with 100 billion tons of recoverable coal, almost 25 percent of our nation's reserves. This is enough to meet our country's need for coal for the next one hundred years and represents more energy content than in the oil in Saudi Arabia and Kuwait combined.

234: Movie Motel

The Sun Motel, on the left just before the overpass, was the setting for a memorable scene in the 1987 movie *Planes, Trains and Automobiles* starring Steve Martin and John Candy. Stranded travelers Neal and Del (Martin and Candy) have to share a bed overnight in room 114 as they make their exhausting journey back home to Chicago for Thanksgiving. Read more about this Hollywood set at 233N.

233: Braidwood Nuclear Power Plant

Situated above one of the many old coal mines in the area, and just down the road from Coal City, the power plant on your left replaces coal with uranium to create electricity. The large white buildings are Exelon Corporation's Braidwood Generating Station. Braidwood is the largest nuclear power plant in Illinois and covers 4,457 acres. It consists of two nuclear reactor units. In 2006, Braidwood's Unit 1 ranked twelfth internationally and first in the United States in output. Together, these two reactors can produce enough power to supply the electricity needs of more than 2 million average American homes. The plant began providing electricity to Chicago and northern Illinois in 1988. With seventeen reactors, Exelon operates the largest fleet of nuclear power plants in the nation.

231: Grundy County

For about twenty miles, Interstate 55 cuts across the southeast corner of Grundy County. William E. Armstrong, the county's bill writer, persuaded officials to name the county for Felix Grundy, a highly acclaimed criminal lawyer of Tennessee whom Armstrong admired. The county was established in 1841, and by 1877, the county directory claimed that Grundy County's "commercial facilities are unsurpassed, having direct communication by railroad and by water with Chicago, the great market of the West, and also with the Mississippi and the Great West beyond." At that time, three railroads and forty-five miles of waterways, including the Illinois River and Illinois & Michigan Canal, passed through the county. Coal and building stone from here traveled to far-off markets, and goods from the eastern U.S. and Europe passed through this county on their long journey to our southern and western states.

230: Ag Country

You are now leaving the urban area and entering a sea of rich, productive cropland. Over the next two hundred miles, you will pass many of Illinois' seventy-six thousand farms. Illinois farms cover more than 28 million acres—nearly 80 percent of the state's land. Illinois is a leading producer of corn, soybeans and hogs. Farmers also grow and raise many other commodities, including cattle, wheat, oats, sorghum, hay, sheep, poultry, fruits and vegetables, as well as specialty products such as alfalfa, canola, horseradish, Christmas trees and even emus and ostriches. The average size of an Illinois farm, including hobby farms, is 368 acres. Most farm acreage is devoted to corn and soybeans. Beef cattle are found on 23 percent of farms, whereas 10 percent of Illinois farms have swine and 3 percent have dairy cows.

With more than 950 food manufacturing companies, food processing is the state's primary manufacturing activity. Most processors are located in the Chicago area, making it one of the largest concentrations of food-related businesses in the world. Illinois ranks second nationally in the export of agricultural products. Illinois farmers help feed the world with more than 44 percent of grain produced in Illinois exported. As you drive past mile after mile of lush croplands, consider how fortunate we are to have land that produces such bountiful harvests that we can then share with hungry people around the world.

228: Fencing the Prairie

On your right, strands of barbed wire run along the top of a modern fence by the frontage road. In the mid-1800s, as early settlers began boxing in the

Illinois prairie with fences, the dense-growing Osage-oranges, or "hedge," became a popular natural fence. Remnants of hedgerows, "horse high, bull strong, and hog tight," still remain in fields throughout the state. At mile 76, you'll pass through a township named for the Osage-orange fences. Lewis H. Thomas built his mansion after he'd planted miles of fence lines with the Osage-orange. Other landowners followed suit, and the tree-lined township became known as Bois D'Arc (French for "bow wood"), another name for Osage-orange trees in recognition that their strong wood made excellent archery bows.

In 1874, a more cost-effective fence for ranchers was invented in Illinois, and Osage-orange wood became sturdy fence posts. Many inventors had experimented with barbed wire fencing, but Joseph Glidden, a farmer from DeKalb, improved an existing model and received a patent for his barbed wirefence design, which became popular around the country. Barbed wire helped settle the American West by keeping the rancher's cattle out of the farmer's cropland and allowing ranchers to manage grazing by moving their cattle between well-defined fenced pastures.

227: Salt Dome

On your left, you'll see a brown dome that looks like it was transported from the set of an intergalactic B-movie. This storage facility is for crystals, not creatures—about 2,700 tons of salt crystals. Dome-shaped buildings are used to store road salt because they efficiently mimic the specific "angle of repose" of a salt pile. The sloping side of a salt pile forms an angle of thirty-two degrees with the ground. This rock salt keeps the roadways safe during snowstorms. If snow is crunching under your wheels, chances are that you're also crunching crystals that came from this dome. The salt from this specific dome is used for nearby roads, including I-55 between miles 217 and 234.

When the National Weather Service announces an approaching storm, the Illinois Department of Transportation (IDOT) will pretreat the road pavement with liquid salt brine. The liquid salt lowers the freezing point of water and keeps dangerous sheets of ice from forming on the highway. IDOT uses the salt to keep the roadway and the ice and snow from forming a bond—not necessarily for melting the snow and ice. As the storm hides the lane lines and disorients drivers, salt trucks fill up with crystals from this dome and head out to slow the process of water turning to ice. For your lane only, it could take up to five hundred pounds of salt to just melt the ice over the next mile. IDOT typically uses more than 500,000 tons of salt on Illinois roadways each winter.

The salt in the storage facility on your right is just like the salt that sits in your pantry or on your dinner table, except that these rock crystals are larger. They will never lose their capability for melting snow and ice, no matter how old they are. And they taste great on pretzels! You'll see another salt dome near mile 55.

224: Power to the People

You might assume that the electricity in the power lines here is coming from the Braidwood nuclear plant a few miles back and is being sent to homes throughout "downstate" Illinois. But in fact, the electricity is flowing north back *toward* the power plant. The power lines crossing the highway ahead bring electricity all the way from the Kincaid Junction Power Plant that you will see south of Springfield at mile 83. It is cheaper to send the energy up here in the form of electricity than shipping the coal here to generate the electricity locally. The electricity in these lines merges and mixes with power produced at other plants to provide light and power to Chicagoland.

Power lines are constructed to carry different amounts of electricity. Voltage is the pressure that moves current through the lines. To move electricity through your home takes 115 volts. About 6,900 volts move power through lines along neighborhood streets. To send power across Illinois requires much bigger lines. The electric line here carries 345,000 volts because it is more efficient to send electricity cross-county at high voltages.

Notice how the cables are spaced far apart and how long insulators are attached the cables to the tower frames. Those insulators are ceramic bells hooked together to ensure that the high voltage will not cause the current to jump across lines. Insulating tape serves this function in household wiring. As the voltage increases, the cables must be farther apart—thus, longer strands of insulators indicate higher voltages. It also takes heavier cables to carry more power. This requires larger towers to support the lines in the face of strong prairie winds.

These towers were designed in the 1960s. Since then, as more power was put into the grid from additional power plants and the new wind farms, the cable "conductors" have begun to sag with the increased load. Concurrently, modern farm equipment has gotten taller. To prevent accidents with farm equipment, Commonwealth Edison used huge cranes to lift these tall towers off the ground and placed ten- to fifteen-foot-tall "inserts" to raise the towers and the wires. Look for towers that have a base that is perpendicular to the ground rather than legs that extend outward. That will indicate that the tower has been raised with an insert. Next time you flip on a switch around your house, consider how far the electricity may have traveled before reaching your home.

221: Delivering Groceries

The large building off to the left is the ALDI Distribution Warehouse. ALDI is an international discount grocery chain with more than one thousand stores in thirty-one states in the Midwest and eastern United States. ALDI also has grocery stores throughout Europe and Australia. This particular warehouse employs about seventy-five people, making it one of Dwight's biggest employers. Read more about the village of Dwight in 216N.

219: Farmstead Forest

Notice the farmstead to the right that is protected by a fortress of trees. All along I-55, you will notice that homes often do not stand alone on this windy, open prairie. Trees provide protection from winds and weather, as well as shade, recreation and beauty. At 181N, read about the many benefits of planting and maintaining a farmstead forest.

218: Slowing the Wind

For the next five miles, you'll see white fences lining the right side of the highway. Just as the wooded tree islands provide windbreaks for farms, these "snow fences" slow the wind and trap snow. The wind empties itself of the blowing snow as its speed slows. The snow fence deposits the snow directly in the path of the additional blowing snow, thereby reinforcing the barrier. Snow fences are easy to install, and they can be made of slats of wood, polyethylene plastic mesh or almost any other material. Some Illinois farmers participate in a low-cost and environmentally friendly project creating "living snow fences" by leaving cornstalks to form windbreaks along highways. In Illinois, snow blows mostly from the west and northwest, so that is why you will only see snow fences on the west (right) side of I-55. While snow fences capture troublesome winds, the huge turbines ahead capture helpful winds.

217: Livingston County

You're in the county of Livingston, I presume. See 187N to learn about this county oddly named after a man not associated with Illinois.

216: Harnessing the Wind

Over the next few miles, you will pass hundreds of wind turbines that animate the prairie sky. In contrast to tree shelterbelts and snow fences, these mighty machines welcome the wind and are gathered into farms that harness the breeze and convert it into hundreds of megawatts that power communities throughout the Midwest. Together, Illinois wind farms produced 3,568 megawatts in 2012. That is enough energy to power about 1.1 million

Huge turbines harness the prairie wind. *LuAnn Cadden.*

homes. Wind energy isn't necessarily new technology—just newer. In 1888, Charles F. Brush constructed the first wind turbine to produce electricity. Towering over his backyard, his windmill powered his Cleveland home.

Recently, wind energy has taken flight as the world tries to power cities with renewable energy. Illinois' wind power will reduce carbon dioxide emissions from coal power plants by 3.5 million metric tons annually. The U.S. Department of Energy has a goal that 20 percent of the nation's energy will be wind-powered by 2030. If you travel all the way down to mile 70, you'll see a single huge wind turbine towering over a backyard. Although Charles Brush's turbine didn't generate as much energy as this one, we're sure they both generated plenty of neighborhood gossip.

213: This Old Barn

While wind turbines are new structures on old farms, some wooden structures still remain. An old barn along the highway is like an old friend. You expect to see them on your travels. Their dependable steadfast presence gives comfort to frequent highway drivers. But barns eventually give way to repeated assaults from tornadic winds and prairie blizzards and from human neglect as newer barns take their place. In *Barns of Illinois*, an I-55 traveler said of this particular barn (at 213), "I pass this barn every time I drive on Interstate 55. I just love this barn, and I'm afraid one day it won't be there."

Most barns were so well built that they last decades even when abandoned. Inevitably, as this book ages, some reader will look up and not see a barn at mile 213. But we hope that some of these old friends will still be there, reminding travelers of a different era of family farming.

210: Predictable Pond Pattern

Natural lakes are scarce in central Illinois, but along the highway, you will notice ponds such as the one here on the right. Pond placement along the highway is predictable. Generally, wherever I-55 crosses over railroads or highways, a pond will be nearby. These ponds were excavated to acquire "fill" to elevate the interstate. After the overpass construction was complete, water filled these holes and created these "interstate ponds." Many have been stocked with fish for private or public fishing, and most provide habitat for migrating waterfowl. Watch for ducks and geese resting on these lakes during spring and fall.

Southbound

207: Bolen's Silo

The concrete silo on the right has the name Robert S. Bolen Stock Farm inscribed on it. Mr. Bolen raised registered Black Angus here from the early 1970s until his death in 1996. Construction of I-55 destroyed the original farmhouse. Robert inherited a trucking business from his father and hauled grain and cattle to market while farming and raising his own cattle. During the 1950s, Robert's father sometimes made five trips per week transporting cattle to the Chicago stockyards. Notice the white patch of paint on the silo. Robert painted an advertisement for the "New Log Cabin Restaurant" in Pontiac that was owned by a friend. The State of Illinois threatened him with a fine for advertising too close to the highway, so he painted over it with the white paint.

Today, the current owners raise corn, soybeans and sheep, but Robert Bolen is still memorialized with this silo. The impressionable silo is mentioned by poet Judith Valente, who also frequently travels this highway. In her poem "Central Illinois, Late October," she lists those familiar landmarks out the window on I-55: "The afternoon drive past Dwight Odell Pontiac Towanda. Familiar markers rise like roadside crosses for the dead: Sun Motel Pete's Harvest Table Robert Bolen Stock Farms."

205: Meramec Barn

If you are driving in the fall or winter, you should be able to see the advertisement for Meramec Caverns painted on the barn ahead on your left. In the early 1930s, Lester B. Dill, the owner of Meramec Caverns in Stanton, Missouri, took a trip to Florida looking for construction work. Along the way, he was impressed by huge advertisements for different products and places that he saw painted on the sides of barns. He decided to use barn painting to advertise the caverns. Read more about these Meramec barns at mile 25.

204: Harvestores

Just ahead, on both sides of the highway, stand tall navy blue silos. These steel silos are Harvestores, a newer model of silo than the concrete one you saw a few miles back. Silos indicate the presence of beef or dairy cattle because they make and store silage, feed for livestock. At harvest

Traveling through Illinois

time, corn or grass can be loaded into the silos and allowed to "ensile" or cure into silage. The glass-lined walls are designed to keep the "fodder," or coarse feed, in an airtight, low-oxygen atmosphere so it can ferment without molding or decaying. You may notice that Harvestore silos have flatter roofs compared to the silver-domed caps of concrete silos. The roof shape reveals the differences in how each type of silo is unloaded. Harvestores are filled from the top and unloaded from the bottom, while cement silos are both loaded and unloaded from the top. The domed roof covers the mechanism, allowing feed to be unloaded down a shoot on the side of the silo. The newest innovation in silos is storing silage in a long white plastic bag that lies along the ground like an enormous white sausage. When a farm is abandoned, some concrete silos are left like tombstones on the prairie. One couple found an innovative way to renovate these old towers and put them to a new use as a rock climbing gym. You can read their story at 159N.

203: No Trash-Passing!

If you are from the Bloomington-Normal or the Chicago area, you may have contributed to the massive mountainous landfill on the right. Allied Waste's Livingston Landfill accepts millions of tons of waste each year from this region. An estimated five thousand tons of trash are dumped here every day. In this area, you are very likely to pass one of the 250 dump trucks that bring their trash here each day.

202: Crop-Dusters

Look to your left at 201.5, and you might see the bright yellow planes of Pontiac Flying Service. To ensure that crops make it into Harvestores and other silos and bins, Scott and Sarah Peterson work to keep the crops well fed and pest-free. They own two "air tractors," and during peak spraying season, they lease up to fifteen other planes and two helicopters from as far away as Kansas to apply fertilizer, fungicides and insecticides to croplands. The term "crop-duster" is a bit archaic, as now most chemicals are applied as liquid rather than powder. The pilots no longer use maps to find the fields and direct their application rates. Instead, they use GPS and computer software, which enhances safety and efficiency.

Sarah emphasized that "no two years are alike." Typically, they begin flying in early spring to apply fertilizer to winter wheat, and then in May, they apply fungicide. In June, Peterson's pilots go to work for the U.S. Forest Service, spraying eastern forests for gypsy moths using a special device patented by Scott. During July, August and September, they will apply pesticides to between 250,000 and 350,000 acres of corn and beans. Obviously, getting fertilizers and pesticides to this many acres through traditional on-the-ground means would be a daunting task, particularly if you had to react quickly to prevent a pest or disease from spreading. If you are traveling I-55 during the summer months, watch for these low-flying airplanes zipping over the fields at 150 to 180 miles per hour.

198: Déjà Vu River

If it seems you've passed over the Vermilion River somewhere else before, it might be because Illinois has two Vermilion Rivers. The one here flows 112 miles north to the Illinois River. The other Vermilion is east of here and flows south through Danville to the Wabash River. Early settlers may have once regarded these two rivers as one since they both drained from wetlands between Pontiac and Danville. Over the years, the headwaters of the two rivers have moved farther apart as wetland areas across the state have been drained for cropland. Native Americans called the river "aramoni," which translated to vermilion and refers to the red clay that Native Americans used to paint their bodies.

195: Riparian Rest

If you'd rather be enjoying a peaceful waterway than crossing over one, you're in luck. At this rest area, you can stretch your legs alongside a wooded stream that seems miles away from a congested highway. The limestone building looks like others on the highway, but if you walk behind the building, you can enjoy a two-story view of nature from the deck or a trek down to the meandering stream and through the surrounding woodlands. This area along the stream is called a riparian corridor. Here, peaceful birdsong replaces backseat bickering, fresh breezes replace stale air conditioning and the bending movement of lush green branches and bushes replace the straight white-lined pavement.

While this riparian rest area is therapeutic for stressed-out drivers, it is also beneficial for wildlife. This patch of forest in a sea of cropland is also a much-needed rest stop for migrating birds. Trees along the stream anchor the soil and keep the water cool and clean. The layer of leaves on the forest floor acts like a sponge, slowing and absorbing water runoff from nearby fields. Leaves fall into the stream and provide the nutrients to start the aquatic food chain. Floating logs are hiding places for fish and basking places for snakes and turtles. The stream-side forest grows tall and fast because the soils are wet and deep. This is a wonderful place to see a few of the Illinois state symbols: the red cardinal, calling his *chip-chip* alarm as you walk by; the spring violets along the forest floor; the white-tailed deer among the oak trees; and possibly the monarch butterfly, as it stops to refuel at unleaded flowers.

189: Faithful Blue Sailors

During the mid- to late summer, you may see "blue sailors" tossing among the grasses. These splashes of bright blue flowers are more commonly known as chicory. Chicory is a common roadside wildflower throughout much of the United States. People have used it as a noncaffeinated coffee substitute. This coffee supplement was especially important in addressing shortages during World War II. The roots can also be used as a vegetable, and the young dandelion-like leaves can be used for salads and potherbs. In much earlier days, a love potion drink was made from chicory to keep a lover faithful. Chicory's nickname, "blue sailors," comes from a story about a beautiful maiden whose lover left her to sail the seas. She waited patiently by the road for so long that the gods took pity on her and changed her into the sailor blue chicory blossom, forever faithful along the roadside.

187: Chenoa

Chenoa comes from the Native American word *chenowa*, which means "white dove." Founder Matthew T. Scott claimed that he named the town Chenowa because it was a native name for his home state of Kentucky, although no records in Kentucky ever confirmed this. In 1856, Scott chose the location for this town because it is where two railroad lines crossed. In the 1800s, railroads were the lifeblood of towns. Generally, towns located on a railroad line thrived, while those that were not near the line died. As highways followed the railroads and connected the dots of railroad towns, Chenoa also became located at the important intersection of US 24 (part of the original U.S. highways system extending from Michigan to Colorado) and historic Route 66.

186: Sunrise, Sunset

Travelers may dismiss this interstate as empty and boring, but this highway through wide-open spaces is the perfect vantage point for amazing sunrises and sunsets. Those who commute through the forested Appalachians or Rockies miss the widescreen showing of a prairie sunset each evening. It moves slowly. Pink light glows on the edges of cumulous clouds and then stretches in a blend of fiery oranges or soft purples. Colors extend and change for miles while darkness creeps from above until the last tiny smear of purple disappears into blackness. No matter the season, I-55 travelers can enjoy a different colorful presentation across the sky every morning and evening. Carl Sandburg spoke of resting in the prairie's embrace: "The prairie sings to me in the forenoon and I know in the night I rest easy in the prairie arms, on the prairie heart." One can imagine that the warm blanket that covered him was the golden sunset setting softly on the prairie.

185: Round Barns

On the right is a beautiful round barn. The first round barn in the United States may have been a barn built by George Washington that had sixteen sides! Round barns were popular from the 1880s until the 1930s because of their efficient design. Farmers could maximize their barn's square footage for the least cost by using the circular or polygon design. Round barns required less wood or stone building material than traditional barns of the same size. Farmers also believed that this design would save steps, and time, in feeding the animals. Another feature was that silos were located inside, usually in the center, so the stored grain wouldn't freeze. Moreover, round barns withstood the blustery prairie winds better than flat barns. The University of Illinois played a big role in making round barns popular in the Midwest. In the early twentieth century, the Agricultural Experiment Station at the university built three round barns. The station was (and still is) influential among farmers. Farmers copied the round designs promoted by the university. In the 1930s, round barns went out of style because as farm equipment got larger, the round barns couldn't expand easily. Also, as time passed, some farmers thought that round barns were more difficult to build than rectangular barns.

184: Cell Towers

Ahead, a cluster of cellphone towers is placed because of the relatively high elevation. Since leaving Chicago, you have been between 550 and 650 feet above sea level. The location of these towers is 737 feet above sea level. You've been climbing the moraine that peaks in Bloomington. (You can read more about this moraine at 142N.) Your ears won't pop from the pressure changes associated with this climb, but for tower placement in this flat landscape, a small difference can be important. Many of us remember the time before cellphone towers lined highways. About 7 million birds are killed annually by colliding with the more than eighty thousand communication towers that have popped up like weeds across North America. The good news is that the trend is to use flagpoles, water towers and even church steeples as cell towers, and for aesthetic reasons, they are sometimes disguised as pine or palm trees, chimneys, streetlamps or other structures. If you see a palm tree in Illinois, you can bet it is a cellphone tower.

182: University Farm

The next generation of farmers and agricultural specialists tend the 360-acre farm on your right. The Illinois State University Farm gives hands-on training, teaching, research and outreach activities for its agricultural and agribusiness students. Located just eighteen miles northeast of campus, students assist a small full-time staff in raising corn, soybeans, alfalfa, swine, beef and sheep.

The university's agriculture program began in 1911, and the first university farm was established in 1912 in the heart of present-day Normal. Ahead at mile 168, you'll see the white crown of Redbird Arena and the Tri-Towers dormitories, where once the farm's crops used to grow. In 1962, the farm moved to Gregory Street, where 250 acres remain. In 2002, the university established the university farm here beyond the confines of the growing city.

This farm produces many benefits. Compost created here is used in local gardens. Several corporations bring employees to the farm to teach them about everything from seeds to safety. Pioneer/DuPont and Mycogen/Dow experiment with new products here. State Farm Insurance Company, headquartered in Bloomington, conducts safety audits here to train their employees. While most farm employees are students, this working farm makes about $500,000 annually. In its fields and barns, young entrepreneurs looking to the future and seasoned professionals honing their craft learn about new and ever-changing practices that will keep Illinois' farming heritage growing.

178: Mackinaw River

Local historians believe that the Mackinaw River was named in honor of a fur trader from Mackinac Island, Michigan, who traded goods along the river. Mackinac Island comes from the Ojibway phrase for "Great Turtle" (Michilimackinac), due to the island's shape. The reason some derivations of the Indian word are Mackinaw (this river and the city in Michigan) and others Mackinac (the island in Lake Huron, the straits, forts and famous bridge) is because French explorers named these sites, and in French, Mackinac sounds like "mack-i-naw," not "mack-i-nack." English-speaking settlers spelled such places Mackinaw with a "w" at the end for correct pronunciation, whereas other places kept the French spelling. Regardless of how you spell it or say it, the Mackinaw River is a lovely 125-mile-long prairie stream that has been the focus of many state and private efforts to preserve its rich plant, fish and wildlife populations.

177: Cattails

In the roadside ditch, you can see a stand of cattails. Cattails need to have "wet feet" during most of the growing season, which is why you find them here in the drainage ditch. Cattails prefer water to be less than eighteen inches deep. Once established, they spread aggressively through their windblown seeds and spreading roots. Cattails provide essential cover and food for birds and other wildlife, unless they are uncontrolled and create stands too dense for animals to use. One of the best things about cattails is that they can filter pollutants out of water and reduce erosion by slowing water in streams and holding shoreline soils intact. The leaves' whitish base tastes like a slightly spicy cucumber. The roots, or tubers, can be used like potatoes. The fluffy seed heads can be used as pancake flour. Settlers used this same fluffy material to stuff pillows and mattresses.

Of course, young boys know the recreational uses for this plant. The furry brown seed heads can be lit like punks on the Fourth of July or be used as pretend cigars, and when the seed heads become white and fluffy, you can whack your friends with them, causing a cloud of seeds to explode and stick all over your victim. Novelist Henry Miller noted, "The moment one gives close attention to anything, even a blade of grass, it becomes a mysterious, awesome, indescribably magnificent thing." Cattails are no exception, and are the "cat's meow" when it comes to being a useful plant.

176: Grain Bins

Silver steel grain bins, like these on the right, are scattered abundantly all along this field-flanked highway. While many grain bins are the typical short, round metal bins with a Tin Man top, these bins sit in a cluster, with individual chutes that meet at the top. To load the bins, the grain is elevated in a bucket up the center shaft and then released down the radiating tubes into the bins. You'll see several more of these interesting connected bins as you continue south.

173: Money Creek

As you pass over this tiny creek ahead, it is unlikely that you will see any coins shimmering in the water, but according to an old story, Indians did find coins in these waters and gave this creek that name. Another story says that an early settler buried some money along this creek that was never found. Supposedly, the settler was a wisecracker who thought it would be funny to tell everyone that he had buried the money but not reveal exactly where it was located. Unfortunately, he died before his secret location was ever disclosed.

172: Towanda

Towanda, another Route 66 town, was established in 1853 and named after Towanda, Pennsylvania, birthplace of Jesse Fell, the founder of Illinois State University and Bloomington, Illinois. Kansas also has a town named Towanda after the same Pennsylvania town.

SOUTHBOUND

171: Duncan Manor

Ahead on your left, at mile 170, you'll see Duncan Manor. The beautiful brick Italianate farmhouse has impressed travelers since 1875 when it was built alongside the Chicago & Alton Railroad. The barn on its left was built just before the house and is the oldest and largest barn in McLean County. Livestock businessman William R. Duncan situated his majestic manor prominently on the hill near the rail lines so that Illinois travelers could admire his stately home. Interstate 55 travelers view the front of the house, but nineteenth-century railroad passengers found the home's back equally impressive. The three-story mansion's triple-thick brick walls have resisted the prairie winds for more than 135 years. These walls harbor the original character of the home's six fireplaces and a thirty-five-foot winding staircase with hand-carved walnut spindles.

In 2000, one I-55 traveler was so spellbound with her first sight of the mansion that she weaved her way off the interstate to see the house that was to become her home seven years later. Diane Sullivan said that the house is her heart, and truly she has put her heart and soul into renovating a historic house that had been a rental property for one hundred years. While renovating, Sullivan tore down a wall to discover a hidden treasure: the thirty-five-foot staircase, in pristine condition. The second floor had been blocked off since the 1940s to retain heat. She also found a cistern, to fill the bathtub, hidden under the second floor in a spot that was incorrectly rumored to have been a secret compartment for slaves traveling the Underground Railroad.

While Mrs. Sullivan has renovated dozens of properties over the years, this home called to her most strongly. Her father's failing health brought her from Florida to Bloomington, and coincidentally, on the same date as her late father's birthday, the house she fought to purchase for years finally became her home. She said that during that eventful, chillingly cold February day, she felt a spiritual closeness to her father, and it became the happiest day of her life. Mrs. Sullivan found that she wasn't the only one who had grown fond of that house over the years. When she opened the house one weekend for a pre-renovation tour, 2,500 travelers, from as far away as Chicago, showed up to enter the home they had marveled at over decades from the lanes of Interstate 55. Everyone seemed to have a story about their affinity for the house. Today, William R. Duncan's mansion continues to impress passing travelers.

TRAVELING THROUGH ILLINOIS

168: Seeing Double

On the left, you'll see the cities of Normal and Bloomington. Bloomington sprouted first in 1831 after a few name changes. Kickapoo Indians found several kegs of whiskey that had been stashed here by early settlers, and that area became known as Keg Grove—long before any university partiers wandered the streets. Then the area became Blooming Grove and finally Bloomington.

The city of Normal grew north of Bloomington when the Illinois State Normal University used the land to build Illinois' first public university. A "normal" school is a school that uses elementary and high school "lab schools" for training student teachers. In 1964, as the university shifted toward the liberal arts, the university dropped the name "Normal" and became Illinois State University (ISU). You may see the white crown of ISU's Redbird Arena and the Tri-Towers dormitories to the left. You can read more about ISU at 161N.

Each city boasts a university. Bloomington's Illinois Wesleyan University (IWU) is tucked in the city center and is not visible from the highway. This liberal arts university was founded seven years before ISU. Its 2,100 students are only blocks away from the 21,000 students in Normal. Notable students of IWU include 1986 graduate Bill Damaschke, the head of animation and creative production for Dreamworks Animation, and comedian Andy Dick. John Belushi, the actor who played the unruly fraternity character John "Bluto" Blutarsky in the movie *Animal House*, applied to IWU. He was not accepted.

163: Mitsubishi

If you're cruising along in a Mitsubishi today, you can look across the field to your right and see the large white building where your car was born. This 636-acre facility is Mitsubishi Motors' only passenger car assembly plant in North America. Since 1988, Diamond Star Motors (the company's original name) has manufactured more than 3 million vehicles behind these walls and exported them to thirty-four countries. Even from your distant view, you can tell that the plant is huge. Just imagine one thousand robots and 1,300 people working under a roof that covers fifty football fields (about 2.4 million square feet) to build vehicles with intrepid names like Endeavor, Avenger, Outlander, Galant and Eagle Talon—vehicles that transport adventurous travelers down roadways around the world.

SOUTHBOUND

160: Cargill

On your left, you'll see the Cargill company logo painted prominently on its facility. As you've driven along today, you have probably seen rows of bushy soybeans in the fields. Here at Cargill, millions of harvested soybeans await the next step in the process of getting from the fields to your pantry.

Founded by William Wallace Cargill in Iowa in 1865, Cargill produces and markets food, agricultural, financial and industrial products in sixty-six countries. This particular facility is a raw material supplier of crude soybean oil and meal. The protein-rich crude oil and meal is then sent on to other Cargill facilities and other companies, where it is refined into products such as vegetable oil, soy milk, flakes, margarine, salad dressing and power drinks. Other nonedible products such as candles, crayons, ink, body lotions, shampoos, hair conditioners, paint removers, fabric conditioners and bio-diesel fuel are also made from soybeans. This facility not only produces soy oil for clean-burning, renewable biodiesel fuel, but it also uses biogas from a nearby landfill in recycling waste into energy. Methane produced from both the landfill and the local wastewater treatment plant produces about 20 percent of the energy used at the Cargill facility. By using the landfill gas, this plant is offsetting the emissions of about four thousand automobiles annually.

157: Sweet Site

On your right is a sweet site: the Nestlé candy manufacturing facility, formerly the Kathryn Beich (pronounced "bike") candy facility. Behind these walls, workers make thousands of sugary confections daily, including Laffy Taffy, Bit-O-Honey and Tollhouse chocolate morsels. Candy has been made in this building since the Beich plant moved here in 1967, but the roots of candy manufacturing in Bloomington go back before the Civil War. In 1854, the J.L. Green Confectionery Company churned out sweets at its factory in downtown Bloomington. In 1892, Paul F. Beich purchased the company that would later become Kathryn Beich. Kathryn Beich is one of the oldest and largest fundraising companies in the United States. You may remember Beich products such as the Whiz Bar, sold during World War II, or chewy Katydid clusters and crunchy Golden Crumbles packaged in tins, or you may remember selling Beich candy for your school, church or sports group.

Beich once offered factory tours. Visitors could work up a sugary appetite watching delicious candies travel along conveyer belts and then satisfy their aching sweet tooth by purchasing discounted broken chocolate pieces and other candies as a finale of their tour. Nestlé bought the Beich Company in 1984 and then sold it to a company from Nashville in 2002. Because of tighter security considerations today, this facility is no longer open to the public. But behind these walls, the candy business still goes on, started by a family that sweetened Bloomington for over a century.

154: Shirley

Not all towns are named after politicians, rich land barons or military officers. In 1857, the town of Shirley was reportedly named by Mrs. Corydon Weed for the heroine in a novel that she was reading. At mile 80 ahead, you will learn about another town named after a character in a novel.

153: Fill 'Er Up with Soy!

Just down the road from where Cargill manufactures soy oil, you'll see on your right signs promoting soy biodiesel: "From Illinois soy bean fields to Illinois roads." As mentioned back at mile 160, soy biodiesel is a clean-burning renewable fuel that is made right here in the United States. Using soy for fuel contributes to the survival of family farms and rural communities and reduces U.S. dependency on foreign oil. While soy is easy on engines, it's also easy on the atmosphere. Soy biodiesel results in 78.5 percent fewer greenhouse gas emissions than petroleum diesel. Illinois farmers produce more than 190 million gallons of biodiesel each year. And Illinois drivers are encouraged to fill 'er up with soy, and they do! More biodiesel is consumed in Illinois than in any other state, partially because Illinois offers a state sales tax exemption for biodiesel blends above 10 percent, making it cheaper than traditional fuel. You'll see more soy signs at mile 148.

150: Halfway There

If you've been traveling from Chicago heading for St. Louis, you're halfway there! The rest area at this mile is two and a half hours between those two cities that begin and end our trip throughout Illinois. The information at this rest area is worth a stop to learn about this historic transportation corridor. Indoor and outdoor exhibits tell stories of early autos, Route 66 and the history of Bloomington-Normal.

Here, you'll also find a marker honoring the Funk family. At this spot in 1826, Isaac Funk built his cabin and began a family farm that still exists today. The Funk farm, located just beyond the forest at this rest stop, has been restored back into a prairie savanna blooming with wildflowers and grasses and has an interpretive nature center, a picnic area and a peaceful outdoor chapel tucked in the woods. The Funk family still sells maple sirup (yes, that's the correct spelling) gathered from the trees that line the road back to the prairie. To visit Funks Grove, take exit 145, and you can read more about the Funk family and their famous sirup at 147N.

148: Making Tracks

At Funks Grove, the Funk family cemetery held a secret for almost 150 years. A large grave holds the remains of about fifty unidentified Irishmen who probably died from cholera while laying the railroad tracks that you see to the right. For the next few miles, the highways of past and present are lined up in parallel transportation aisles. You are traveling a highway of the 1960s, the one to the right of you was the highway of the 1930s and the one to the right of it was the highway of the 1850s. In 1847, the Alton & Sangamon Railroad (later named the Chicago & Alton) began laying tracks from St. Louis to Springfield. By 1853, those tracks had reached Bloomington.

An Irish rail workers' memorial in the Funks Grove cemetery. *LuAnn Cadden.*

Most of the men and boys who labored to make this road for the "iron horse" were from Ireland. They traveled together, shared stories and songs while they worked and shared their meals and living quarters in crowded boxcars. It may have been these crowded conditions that aided the rapid spread of disease that killed many men within just a few days. Small towns nearby were frightened to allow the infectious bodies into their community, but the Funk family invited the railroad to bury the men in their own family plot just north of where the men had died. For years, the grave was covered over and never marked because they had no names to put on it. But on Worker's Memorial Day, April 28, 2000, the McLean County Historical Society and citizen donations divulged the secret resting place. In the Funk family cemetery, they placed a Celtic cross monument to recognize those anonymous men "whose sacrifices opened interior Illinois and made it possible to develop the riches of the land we share today." Jesse Fell, the famous businessman in Bloomington, recognized the rails as "the road of the state":

> *How can it be otherwise when we reflect that Chicago on the one hand, and St. Louis on the other, are the great commercial centers of this part, if not indeed of the whole Mississippi Valley; and that this road will constitute the nearest practicable connection between those two great cities? Looking at it from this point of view alone…the Chicago & Alton road assumes an importance that does not attach to any other road.*

As you pass "Men at Work" signs on Interstate 55, remember all the hundreds of hands that helped build this transportation timeline spanning more than 150 years, drove spikes into sturdy oak ties, laid the first concrete lanes across the prairie, grated the roads and painted lines on the federal highways crossing Illinois.

145: Dixie Truckers Home

The Dixie Truckers Home at exit 145 was a family-owned business that really did operate as a "home" for travelers for seventy-five years. During the depression years, those who came here were never turned away hungry. At 144N, read more about this establishment that has served travelers since Route 66.

SOUTHBOUND

142: Prairie State

Along the roadside ahead, a sign reads, "Prairie grass restoration Next 101 Miles!" When settlers ventured into what would become Illinois, the prairies opened up before them in a sea of wildflowers and grasses. While Indiana and Ohio had some prairie habitat, never before had easterners witnessed such large expanses of grassland. The slightest wind could keep the waves of grass perpetually bending, swaying and rolling all the way to the horizon. Some prairies consisted of towering big bluestem grass, whose turkey foot-shaped seed heads could reach up to ten feet tall. Other prairies were a mixture of grasses and wildflowers that firmly dug their roots as far as fifteen feet deep into the soil. Today, the Illinois Department of Transportation is restoring the beauty and benefits of prairies along I-55 through central Illinois.

In 1820, native prairie covered two-thirds of Illinois. By the 1950s, the decade in which I-55 was paved, less than 1 percent of the original 22 million acres remained. When the lanes of I-55 dissected the prairie state, 139,000 acres of roadsides were created. In the late 1960s, IDOT began to use these roadsides to bring back the prairie. Beautiful, beneficial and low-maintenance, the deep roots of wildflowers keep themselves well watered, hardy and tolerant of the summer's scorch. Today, IDOT, with the help of the Illinois Natural History Survey's Prairie Research Institute, keeps an inventory of roadside prairie plants in order to protect them from destruction. In these restoration areas, you may glimpse the Illinois state insect, the monarch butterfly, feeding on nectar or laying its eggs on milkweed or see the Illinois state grass, big bluestem.

140: Logan County

You have entered Logan County. At mile 112N, you can read about this county, which Abraham Lincoln named after his friend.

139: Have a Nice Day!

On your right, a yellow water tower with a smiley face rises above Atlanta, which rose to prominence as a railroad town and then as a Route 66 town. This quiet place was once a bustling boomtown. Crops and livestock from prosperous farms were shipped to Chicago, bringing people and wealth to

Traveling through Illinois

Smiling over Atlanta. *LuAnn Cadden.*

Atlanta. Newspapers of the day raved about Atlanta. A reporter for the *Alton Courier* reported, "Of all the towns it has been my fortune to visit, since I have been in the rambling trade, Atlanta possesses the largest share of the young American spirit of progressiveness. It is the largest town of its age I have ever seen…the amount of business that is done is immense…The citizens are intelligent, sociable and hospitable."

This statement may have portended the happy face on the water tower. Even a reporter from the *Chicago Tribune* was impressed with Atlanta, writing, "Before I visited this renowned place…I almost came to the conclusion that it had only been represented on the bright side, but I confess that I was surprised to find so much of a town and so much done here in the way of business."

Abraham Lincoln gave an address at the 1859 Fourth of July celebration here and also rehearsed for one of his debates with Stephen Douglas here. It seems fitting that a town at the center of Illinois would have a history woven with stories of rich farmland, railroads, Route 66 and Abe Lincoln—all iconic symbols of Illinois.

Southbound

136: Through the Eyes of 66ers

On those Route 66 trips through Atlanta, southbound travelers (like you) would pass over the original stone bridge on your right. Their old jalopy wheels were framed by the vase-like baluster spindles that you can still see today. The 66ers would travel on past the historic Lawndale grain elevator with an original Faultless Feed advertisement that still remains. The Faultless Milling Company began producing animal feed in Springfield in 1881, and now its feedbags are collectors' items.

135: The First Lincoln

Many counties, towns, parks and schools are named for Abraham Lincoln, but this town you are approaching is the only one named for him *before* he became president of the United States. The city's Lincoln College is also the only institution of higher education named for Abraham Lincoln during his lifetime. It became Lincoln University on February 6, 1865. The founders named this city after the Springfield lawyer who helped them incorporate their new town. Replying to the honor, in his always witty and often humble way, Lincoln said, "I think you are making a mistake. I never knew anything named Lincoln that ever amounted to much." On August 27, 1853, the first public lots were sold with the legal assistance of the amiable attorney. By the end of that first day, ninety plots, varying from $40 to $150, had been purchased. In a ceremonious gesture, forever to elevate the status of a simple melon, Lincoln took a cup of watermelon juice, poured it on the soil and christened the town in his own Lincoln-esque style. Today, in downtown Lincoln, you can find a slice of metal watermelon forever situated to commemorate the birth of this area, the first of many places to be honored with the name Lincoln—a name that certainly amounted to much.

133: Weather Radar

The white ball on the left horizon houses a National Weather Service Doppler radar. This weather radar, one of 155 in the United States, is located at the Logan County Airport. This particular radar was commissioned in 1996, but radar has been used to detect rain and snow since the 1940s. Modern Next Generation Radars (NEXRAD) emit bursts of energy. When the energy strikes a raindrop, some of the energy is directed back toward the radar. The radar emits a signal, listens for a returned signal and then emits the next signal up to 1,300 times each second. Computers analyze the returned energy to determine the type, location and movement of the objects struck by the signal. This allows meteorologists to see inside thunderstorms and determine if there is cloud rotation, often a precursor to tornado formation. These return signals are so sensitive that echoes from migrating birds or swarms of bats can appear on the radar screen. Doppler radars like this one have saved many lives by tracking the movement of dangerous storms, thereby allowing people time to take shelter.

131: Conestoga Commerce

It's a Conestoga! It's a prairie schooner! It's...a covered wagon! As you pass the town of Lincoln, imagine the covered wagons that once traveled this route. Walnut and oak wheels lifted the entire vehicle on every pebble, the onward march of oxen and horses created a never-ending swirl of dust and the sun burned the driver while others walked along or rested under the wagon's cotton bonnet. In downtown Lincoln, you can see the world's largest covered wagon, as noted by *Guinness World Records*. It weighs five tons and measures forty feet long, twelve feet wide and twenty-four feet tall. The town's namesake, Abraham Lincoln (all twelve feet tall and 350 pounds of him), holds the reins. But is his wagon a prairie schooner or a Conestoga? Both were covered wagons in the mid-1800s, but each had its own design and purpose.

The Conestoga was the semi-trailer of the day. First built in the 1700s, the largest Conestogas were fourteen- to sixteen-foot-long freighters built solid, with a floor that was sloped in the middle to keep barrels and other goods secure. It took six large horses (or a dozen oxen) to pull its weight, which was sometimes six thousand pounds, and its rear wheels were as tall as the men who drove it. Conestogas had no front seat. The driver would either ride the wheel horse (the horse on the left side closest to the wagon) or the lazy board (a board attached to the wagon's left side). Interestingly, the American placement of the driver on the left side of the car supposedly originated because of the Conestoga. Being the largest vehicle on the road, it had the right of way, and with the driver on the left, all others had to pass on that side.

As settlers moved out on the Oregon Trail, they realized that the Conestoga wasn't the best set of wheels to cruise across the country. It was better suited for the commerce-heavy Santa Fe Trail. Thus, the prairie schooner was born, a bit smaller and lighter and only requiring four to six oxen to pull the family and their essentials for the long trip to find a new home. From these clues, you just may have figured out whether the world-record covered wagon is a Conestoga or a prairie schooner, but to see it for yourself, you can stop off in downtown Lincoln and check it out.

126: Have You Seen It?

Today's Conestogas are trucks, like the Federal Express ones on your left at the Federal Express Freight Center. A FedEx truck is a common sight along the interstate—not really worth a second look, right? But take that second look at its logo. Between the "e" and "x," you'll see a white arrow. It represents a "forward-moving" company. Creative graphic designers sometimes imbed visuals with deeper meanings in their logos. The CEO of Conoco was from the University of Oklahoma, and if you flip the lowercase letters "c" and "n," you'll see that you can make each of them into a "u." So, all the letters in the Conoco logo are either an "o" or a "u," in honor of the CEO's alma mater. Many car companies have interesting logos. One of these is BMW. The white triangles represent the propeller of a plane in motion, and the blue triangles are the sky. This emphasizes that BMW once built engines for German military planes. Some snacks you're munching on today may also have a hidden message within them. The mountain on a Toblerone chocolate bar is apparent, but have you seen the bear disguised in the mountain? A dancing bear silhouette is in the center of the mountain because Toblerone was from Bern, Switzerland, also called the "City of Bears." You may notice more hidden logos on your I-55 journey, but you may never look at another FedEx truck in the same way again.

124: I See a Hippopotamus

Clouds can be the constellations of the daytime sky. Above you are shapes and stories in ever-changing forms. With a little imagination, you might see a tiger's huge claw reaching out for a rabbit with a cumulus cottontail or horses with cirrus manes swept back in the wind racing for the wispy flag at the finish line. The skies can be much more than stories if you know how to read the clouds. Since 1803, thanks to English pharmacist Luke Howard, we've been able to classify clouds into puffball cottony "cumulus"; thin, wispy "cirrus"; and straight, stretchy "stratus." From those Latin roots, several other types of clouds can be named (e.g., cirrostratus or cumulonimbus). The wispy "mare's tail" can indicate that a cold front is moving in, while fish scales can indicate a warm front. Cumulus clouds that dot the sky like a field of cotton mean fair weather, whereas the majestic anvil-shaped tops of cumulonimbus clouds, or "thunderheads" (some reaching fifty thousand feet in the atmosphere and containing as much energy as a nuclear bomb!), indicate violent weather.

Can you see any airplanes flying at least twenty-five thousand feet above today? At this altitude, planes actually make cirrus clouds in the sky. The smoky-looking contrails that stream behind a plane are ice crystals created from water vapor from the plane's engines. Because these clouds were created from adding moisture to the air, their longevity in the sky can predict the weather. If a contrail stays in the air for a while, it indicates moisture in the air and could mean that precipitation is coming. If a contrail quickly vanishes, then the air is drier and it should be a fair weather day.

Clouds are both beautiful and interesting. Members of the Cloud Appreciation Society believe that "clouds are expressions of the atmosphere's moods, and can be read like those of a person's countenance." Cloud-watching should be considered an official sport on wide-open interstates like I-55. Until that happens, read the clouds like a weather forecast and keep enjoying the stories found in the heavens.

120: Broadwell

The former northbound lanes of Route 66 remain intact and still serve as a local road in Broadwell. Along this road, the Pig Hip Restaurant, operated by Ernie Edwards from 1937 through 1991, was a popular stopping point for folks "on the road to Chicago." The Pig Hip ham sandwich, served with Ernie's secret sauce, was a favorite menu item. Ernie once received the citation for the "Best U.S. Route 66 attraction where the ORIGINAL GUY is still there." Between 1991 and 2007, the Pig Hip building was a museum of Route 66 memorabilia, with Ernie serving as host. Although fire destroyed the restaurant/museum building on March 5, 2007, Ernie's family and friends wouldn't let it be forgotten. On August 5, 2007, the occasion of Ernie's ninetieth birthday, they unveiled a stone and bronze memorial to the Pig Hip Restaurant and Route 66. You can see this memorial by taking exit 115.

SOUTHBOUND

The Pig Hip Restaurant and the Elkhart Grain Company. *LuAnn Cadden.*

118: Elkhart Grain Company

Directly ahead, the Elkhart Grain Company's silos rise like a castle. If grain elevators are the castles of the prairie, then the Elkhart Grain Company rules this kingdom. With this grain elevator, one in Broadwell and one each in Mount Pulaski and Lake Fork, the company has the capacity to store more than 7 million bushels of grain. At this elevator, it can store 3.5 million bushels. Farmers from a ten-mile radius bring their corn, soybeans and wheat from about sixty thousand acres of cropland to this site. From here, some grain is shipped by truck to destinations like Archer Daniels Midland Company (ADM) in Decatur, where the company converts it into products for food, animal feed, chemical and energy uses. Other grain is shipped by a seventy-five-car unit train to feed chickens in Texas and Arkansas. You have a few chances per month to see the grain trains roll from this facility in its parallel route to I-55.

TRAVELING THROUGH ILLINOIS

116: Elkhart

This village of 450 people at the base of Elkhart Hill was called Elk Heart Grove, then Elk Heart City, then Elkhart City and finally, in 1979, just Elkhart. The legend of how the hill, and hence the town, got its name states that a Kickapoo chief's daughter, White Blossom, was wooed by two warriors, one from her own tribe, the Illini, and another from the Shawnee tribe from Ohio. When an elk passed by, White Blossom said that she would choose for her husband the one who could pierce the elk's heart with his arrow. The warrior from the Kickapoo tribe hit the heart of the elk, and when they married, the elk heart became their family symbol.

Noteworthy people who lived in Elkhart included John Dean Gillette, who moved here in 1838 and amassed large amounts of land and livestock. Gillette is famous for developing the Shorthorn cattle breed. He shipped thousands of head of cattle and hogs to Europe and became known as the "Cattle King of the World." He was friends with and a business associate of Lincoln's, and they both courted the same woman, who later became Gillette's wife. Another famous resident was Richard Oglesby, a Civil War hero and three-time governor. Oglesby also was a close friend of Lincoln's and suggested the "railsplitter" name for the 1860 presidential campaign. Oglesby had the last business appointment with Lincoln on the day that he was assassinated. In fact, he was invited to go along to Ford's Theater that night but declined. After the shooting, he was called to Lincoln's deathbed, and he appears in the famous painting of the dying president. Oglesby helped raise funds for Lincoln's tomb and gave the address at the tomb's dedication. A.H. Bogardus, a world champion marksman credited with creating the sport of skeet shooting, also lived here and frequently hosted Buffalo Bill Cody in his home.

112: Sangamon County

In one mile, you'll enter Sangamon County. In 1817, Robert Pulliam built the first pioneer settlement of Sangamon County just south of Springfield. Pulliam was a Virginia native who established a string of settlements as he slowly made his way west and finally found the Sangamon Valley, a lush landscape of streams, forests and prairie. Governor John Reynolds (1831–34) wrote that "Sangamon County became famous and known all over the west as the most beautiful country in the valley of the Mississippi. It acquired a great reputation, as it deserved, for its exceedingly fertile soil and fine timber, which last advantage attracted a numerous, respectable, and wealthy population from Kentucky." Ahead, you'll have the opportunity to cross the Sangamon River (mile 103) and exit on Sangamon Avenue (mile 100).

108: Funeral Train

During your journey, you may have seen a passenger or freight train traveling between Chicago and Springfield on these rails paralleling I-55. On May 3, 1865, the most memorable train in Illinois history passed along this same route. President Abraham Lincoln's funeral train brought him home to Springfield. When Lincoln left Springfield on February 11, 1861 (the day before his fifty-second birthday), he stood at the train depot and bid his friends a sad farewell:

> *Friends, no one who has never been placed in a like position can understand my feelings at this hour, nor the oppressive sadness I feel at this parting. For more than a quarter of a century I have lived among you, and during all that time I have received nothing but kindness at your hands. Here I have lived from my youth until now I am an old man. Here the most cherished ties of earth were assumed. Here all my children were born and here one of them lies buried. To you, dear friends, I owe all that I have, all that I am... With these words I must leave you—for how long I know not. Friends, one and all, I must now bid you an affectionate farewell.*

Four years later, a train brought him back to the Springfield depot, once again among tearful friends. On April 21, 1865, the funeral train left Washington and began its 1,700-mile journey to Springfield. Several million mourners, with bowed heads and teary eyes, waited alongside the tracks for their moment to pay respects to him as the train passed. In the late evening of May 2, the train left Chicago and followed the future route of I-55. In Joliet, Bloomington and Lincoln, large silent crowds had gathered, and in the smaller towns, hundreds more mourners lined the tracks, sometimes illuminating the route with torches held high and sometimes even paying tribute with funeral arches placed over the tracks. The town of Williamsville, which you've just passed, had an arch that said, "He has fulfilled his mission."

Traveling through Illinois

Lincoln's funeral train pulling into Springfield. *Sangamon Valley Collection, Lincoln Library.*

On the morning of May 3, the train moved slowly into Springfield, taking two hours to go about a mile and a half. The *New York Tribune* reported that

> *The pall-bearers, those old men, friends of his, lang syne, approach. The stillness among all the people is painful; but when the coffin is taken from the car, that stillness is broken, broken by sobs, and these are more painful than the stillness. The coffin is borne to the hearse; the hearse moves slowly, almost tenderly, away, followed by the mourners, and the pallbearers walk by the side. The cortege, more solemn than any that had gone before, reaches the States House, where he was wont to speak face to face with his neighbors—where at this hour those neighbors press to behold his face locked in death. All night they will pass by with eyes searching through tears for resemblances and recognition of the features they knew so well.*

103: Crossing the Sangamon

Ahead, you'll cross the Sangamon River, the river that brought a twenty-one-year-old Abraham Lincoln to settle in New Salem, just west of here.

Southbound

During Lincoln's years from 1831 to 1837 at New Salem, he lived along this river and navigated it by flatboat. Read more about this historic river at 102N.

102: Springfield, a "Capital" City

Springfield is home to 120,000 people and almost as many stories about its most famous resident, Abraham Lincoln. Here is where Lincoln shared a law office, moved into his first home with Mary Todd, raised his boys, learned that he had been elected the sixteenth U.S. president, delivered an emotional farewell address before leaving for the White House and returned four years later on a funeral train to be buried in his beloved city.

Those not schooled well on their state capitals may mistake metropolitan Chicago as the seat of Illinois government. The joke in Illinois is that any city south of the Chicago Metro Area is located in "southern Illinois." Chicago actually might have been the Illinois capital if it weren't for the Great Fire in 1871. The General Assembly had planned to convene in the Windy City, but the fire necessitated their return to Springfield, and the construction of a new capitol proceeded in "southern Illinois."

101: All Eyes on the Capitol

As you near the Sangamon Avenue overpass at mile 100, you will get your first glimpse of the silver capitol dome ahead and to the right. The dome is to the right of the tall Hilton Hotel. Read about the "sky wars" between the capitol and the Hilton at 90N. Illinois' capitol building is the tallest domed capitol in the United States, even taller than the U.S. Capitol (288 feet) in Washington, D.C. From its first floor to its dome, the Illinois capitol rises 361 feet, and the flag waves 405 feet above the city.

The capital seat was moved from Vandalia to Springfield in 1837. In 1888, this capitol building opened its doors. Just a few blocks away, tourists can also tour the smaller, but still impressive, Old State Capitol. The death of its first architect delayed construction, but W.W. Boyington, the designer of Chicago's Water Tower building, completed the project twenty years after it first began. Gas jets numbering 144 illuminated the dome when it first opened, but years of burning carbon turned the interior black. In 1986, the dome was cleaned to restore its original brilliance. During the Christmas

Traveling through Illinois

The Springfield capitol, decorated for the 1907 state fair, with beacon flashing. *Sangamon Valley Collection, Lincoln Library.*

season, long strands of lights cascade outward from the red-tipped capitol top and resemble a gigantic Christmas tree.

Years ago, eyes weren't focused on the capitol only during the Christmas season. According to former Springfield police officers who served in the 1930s and '40s, officers kept their eyes on the capitol dome. Before police radios, a blinking beacon flashed from the top of the dome to alert officers that there was an emergency. When a problem was called in to the police station, they would flip a switch on and off, and like Batman's bat symbol lit high above Gotham City, police officers would see the signal and call in from a callbox to see how they could help.

98: Prairie Power

Springfield's other tall structures loom ahead on your left: the smokestacks of the City, Water, Light and Power (CWLP) plant. So many children have curiously asked about the white fluffy smoke pluming from these stacks that a Facebook site was dedicated to the thought ("I used to think that CWLP towers were cloud makers when I was a kid"). Coal, fuel oil and natural gas units combine to create up to 698 megawatts. Most of that power is generated purely by Illinois coal extracted from state mines like the Viper Mine at 111N. In 2010, the four coal-fired units used almost 14 million tons of coal. Just past the facility, on your left, you can see a tiny inlet of Lake Springfield, which was completed in 1935 so that Springfield's earlier power plant, located on the Sangamon River, could be moved here in 1936. The shorter black stack that isn't smoking was the plant's original smokestack. You can read more about Lake Springfield at mile 89N.

93: Famous Fair Food

Just ahead, before I-55 veers to the left toward St. Louis, take the Sixth Street exit to get a batter-covered frankfurter at the Cozy Drive-In, historic home of the first corn dog on a stick. Sixth Street was once Business Route 66, and less than a mile from this exit on the left, you can still dine at this icon of the "Mother Road" and see Route 66 pamphlets, postcards and maps. While visiting Oklahoma, Ed Waldmire had his taste buds and entrepreneurial spirit inspired by a hot dog baked in cornbread. Though delicious, he thought he could improve it. A baker gave Waldmire a recipe for batter that would stick to the dog snuggly while it was being

Cozies at the Cozy Drive-In. *LuAnn Cadden.*

fried. In 1945, while in the U.S. Army Air Corps, Waldmire first tested his new creation on his military pals. He then returned to Springfield, where he introduced his "cozy dog" (named by his wife). In 1946, the state fair began selling them, and they are still a favorite at fairs everywhere.

Traveling through Illinois

92: Sensory Experience

In the distance on your right, you can see the colorful tops of playground equipment and the tall wind turbine at Edwin Watts Southwind Park. This park is one of the nation's most innovative parks for people with cognitive and physical disabilities. Tactile signs, color-coded trails, flower and vegetable gardens and a playground all surpass the minimum requirements of the Americans with Disabilities Act. The eighty-acre park is still being developed and will include a Splash Fountain, sports courts and a three-thousand-seat amphitheater. The wind turbine, along with solar panels and geothermal power, generate energy for Erin's Pavilion, an indoor space named for Erin Elzea, whose enzyme deficiency restricted her to a wheelchair until her passing at the age of seventeen.

91: Pork Poems, Swine Sonnets and Bacon Ballads

On your left (mile 90) is the Illinois Pork Producers Association (IPPA). Here you'll find recipes such as "Bacon and Peanut Butter Cookies," poems about pigs and statistics on swine to help support a mission "to provide pork producers with services that enhance profitability and consumer preference for pork." Illinois is fourth in the nation in pork production, and the IPPA represents more than 2,900 producers who raise 8.3 million pigs per year. Their work branches out to affect more than 18,500 jobs in feed and equipment, transportation and processing. Because pigs "eat like hogs," they also benefit Illinois grain producers by consuming 94 million bushels of corn and 28 million bushels of soybeans per year.

IPPA promotes pork in interesting ways—racing pigs at the state fairgrounds, donating pork to the poor through "Pork Power" and penning poems to pork at Chicago's Baconfest. Even America's "Uncle Sam" may have had a direct relation to the pork industry. Stories say that Sam Wilson was a meat inspector who, during the war of 1812, shipped several hundred barrels of pork to U.S. troops. Because each barrel was stamped with "U.S.," it was said that Uncle Sam had sent the provisions.

89: Lincoln Memorial Garden

Exit 88 will take you to the Lincoln Memorial Garden, an area of trails that wander through oaks, maples, hickories, wildflowers and grasses along the edge of Lake Springfield. In 1936, just after the lake was built, Springfield resident Harriet Knudson suggested creating a living memorial to Abraham Lincoln along the lake's shore—a place where people could be surrounded by the native plants that Lincoln would have seen when he lived in Kentucky, Indiana and Illinois. Jens Jensen, a renowned landscape architect and associate of Frank Lloyd Wright, designed the original sixty-three acres as "not an arboretum, not a collection of plants, but a pure symphony of living beauty." Jensen chose an area of farm fields with a few trees and a winding stream to transform into lush foliage-lined paths. On November 14, 1936, Scouts planted the first acorns that have grown into the enormous oaks that shade the paths today.

Today, the garden spreads over more than one hundred acres and has six miles of trails, with footbridges that cross over a stream, wooden benches inscribed with Lincoln quotes, a nature center and gift shop and the twenty-nine-acre Ostermeier Prairie Center. Although Lincoln was never known to walk this area, he would have recognized the maples with their fiery color in fall and sugary sap of winter, the spring beauties (*Claytonia*) that dot the woodland floor and the strong branches of the oaks that stretch out in the summer sun.

87: The Gift that Kept on Giving

You've entered back into agricultural land and are passing fields that rotate between corn and soybeans. Back at mile 160, we mentioned specific gifts that soy gives us, from fuel to food to fabric conditioners; the seed that sprouted them truly was a gift. Originally cultivated in China, the soybean first took root on U.S. soil in 1765 in Savannah, Georgia. In the 1850s, the soybean finally arrived in the fertile Midwest by an unusual route and the serendipitous meeting of two people at the right place and the right time.

In 1850, a cargo ship left Hong Kong for San Francisco, encountered on the way a ship of Japanese fishermen who were ill and took them aboard. But after the long trip to San Francisco, the fishermen were not allowed to step onto U.S. soil because of their illness. By chance, Dr. Benjamin Franklin Edwards was waiting to board a passenger ship that would take him back to Alton, Illinois, via the Panama Overland route, and he offered to examine the men. He found that the illness was not contagious, and the men were allowed on land. In their immense gratefulness, the foreign fishermen gave the American doctor a gift of what they had with them: soybeans.

Traveling through Illinois

Dr. Edwards returned to Alton and passed his gift to his horticulturist friend, John H. Lea. In 1851, the first Illinois soybean broke through the earth in Lea's garden. From Illinois, Lea passed his seeds to farmers in Davenport, Iowa, and Cincinnati, Ohio. From Ohio, the seed descendants were passed to the New York State Agricultural Society, the Massachusetts Horticultural Society and the commissioner of patents. These organizations then sent seeds to dozens of farmers throughout the United States. By the late 1850s, news of the soybean's value had spread throughout the country, and a simple gift for an act of kindness had multiplied into a multitude of gifts that we enjoy today.

84: Getting to the Source

Just ahead, way in the distance to your left, the Kincaid Power Plant rises from the horizon. This coal-fired plant generates 1,158 megawatts, enough power for 290,000 homes. The plant, owned by Dominion Resources, was built in 1967. As mentioned back at mile 224, electricity from this plant travels in power lines all the way back north to the Chicago area to help provide light and energy to homes and business there.

83: Lake Sangchris

Power plants require enormous amounts of water to be heated and turned into steam to turn the turbines. That is why they are invariably located along rivers and lakes. Just as Lake Springfield provides water to the power plant there, so does Lake Sangchris, built in 1964, provide water for the Kincaid Power Plant. Such cooling lakes greatly benefit nearby communities, particularly in central Illinois, where lakes and water recreation opportunities are scarce. With 120 miles of shoreline and 3,022 acres of land, Sangchris Lake State Park offers fishing, boating, hunting, camping, hiking and picnic shelters. In winter, the warm waters that flow back out from the power plant keep ice off the lake, thereby allowing both anglers and eagles to fish year round. Sangchris Lake was named for the two counties into which it extends: Sangamon and Christian.

82: From Pump to Pump

On the right, just before and after the overpass, horses of a different kind work in the fields. Three pump jacks, also called "horsehead pumps," pull oil from the earth. By looking at the shape of the lever, you can see where these pumps get their nickname. Their shape and movement have also inspired the nicknames of "nodding donkeys," "grasshopper pumps" and "thirsty birds" (our favorite), among several others. Each stroke brings up a cup or two of fluid (oil-water mixture). Most wells are about half a mile deep, but some pumps pull oil from thirteen thousand feet below the surface. A "prime mover" (an electric motor or combustion engine) works with cranks, pulleys and rods to start the journey of oil from this pump to the pump at the gas station.

Illinois has about thirty thousand wells on 650 oil fields that produce 10 to 12 million barrels of oil per year. In the early 1860s, one of Illinois' first oil wells was drilled in Montgomery County, which you just passed through. Of 102 counties in Illinois, 40 produce oil. In southern and central Illinois, many farmers harvest energy from above and below ground. Oil formed

Pump jack pulling oil from the earth. *LuAnn Cadden.*

TRAVELING THROUGH ILLINOIS

from prehistoric plants and animals, which captured and converted sunlight eons ago, flows underground, while corn and soy now prosper above ground. Whether you are using biofuels or traditional fuel, in a very real sense, your car is running on solar energy stored as chemical energy in your gas tank.

80: Divernon

Just like the town of Shirley, back at mile 154, the little town of Divernon was named for a fictional character. In 1887, resident H.C. Barnes named the town for Diana Vernon, the heroine of Sir Walter Scott's 1817 novel *Rob Roy*. Read more about "Di" Vernon at 79N.

76: Mysterious Mansion

Many intriguing stories have been told about the impressive brick mansion on your left. The phrase "if walls could talk" perfectly describes the intrigue that this

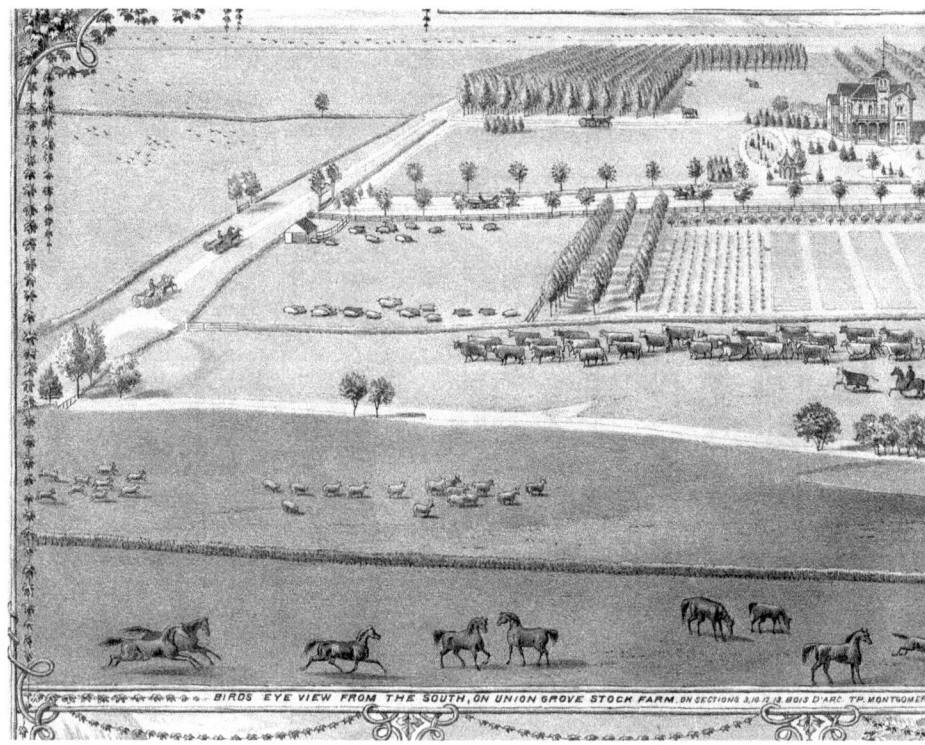

house has aroused in local communities. Folklore claims that it was a stop on the Underground Railroad or a hangout for mobsters traveling between Chicago and St. Louis. Others simply talk about ghosts in the haunted house. The house design wasn't sketched out until 1863, the same year that the Emancipation Proclamation freed slaves. That likely rules out the Underground Railroad, but as for the other stories, who knows? However, historians do know about the man who first lived in this beautiful home and the home's extravagant beginnings.

In 1851, Lewis Thomas's estate covered these interstate lines and spread out for 970 acres across Montgomery County. Before he built this mansion, he established natural fences and timber groves on the estate. His use of Osage-orange trees as a hedge fence encouraged other landholders to do the same, and eventually, hedgerows became so popular that they named the growing township Bois D'Arc (French for "bow wood").

His estate became known as the Union Grove Stock Farm, where they managed horses, sheep, cattle, hogs and chickens along with other atypical farm

Below: The Lewis Thomas Union Grove Stock Farm, 1874. Today, I-55 runs along the west side of the house. *From the* Illustrated Atlas of Montgomery County, Illinois.

animals such as peacocks, deer and bears. This impressive estate even had its own boardwalk connecting it directly to the Illinois Central Railroad station that was built just west of his home. Thomas lived here until his death in 1909, and since then, this prairie queen has been a private home and a bed-and-breakfast.

Today, the timber groves have been removed for farming and the Osage-orange hedgerows have been replaced by modern fences. The only remnants of Thomas's impressive estate are the grain elevators from his Thomasville Grain Company and the mysterious mansion that holds its stories within its walls.

73: Wind Power

If you've traveled from Chicago, you've seen wind farms populated with hundreds of turbines spinning wind into energy. But on the left, only one wind turbine works to harness the breeze. The towering windmill is named the Gob Knob turbine since it was constructed on a "gob pile," an area where coal was discarded. In 2009, it began producing 4 to 5 percent of the power supply for Rural Electric Convenience Cooperative, based in Auburn. It needs at least a four-mile-per-hour wind to operate and shuts down at wind speeds of fifty-five miles per hour and higher to avoid damage to the turbine.

68: Life in a Small Town

Ahead at mile 67, you'll see an old wooden sign welcoming you to Waggoner. Have you ever wondered what life is like in these small towns along the highway? Peggy Hampton, who grew up in Waggoner and still lives nearby, said that growing up in Waggoner was "safe and slow paced." She has fond memories of watching movies outside on Main Street on summer nights and being surrounded by friends and family.

Waggoner is a close-knit community. When neighbors are ill, townspeople raise money to help with medical costs or tend their farm fields until they heal. They play BINGO and eat turkey dinners at the American Legion Hall. Most people work in Springfield or Litchfield. In the mornings and evenings, people walk for exercise along the cornfield-flanked rural roads or ride bikes on the Rails-to-Trails trail linking Waggoner with Farmersville. Children compete with youth from neighboring towns in sports or participate in church youth group activities.

Southbound

Welcoming travelers to Waggoner. *LuAnn Cadden.*

George and Elizabeth Waggoner gave part of their farmland to form the village in 1886. The town prospered until the early 1970s, when the interstate offered travelers an exit to Farmersville rather than Waggoner. Over time, the grocery store, grain elevator, mechanics garage, bank and two of the three churches folded up. In 1986, even their grade school closed due to low enrollment, casting a pall on the town's centennial year. The town preserved the old school and converted it to a community center, aptly named the Centennial Building.

Many rural towns rally around an annual local event. In 1988, to raise money for the maintenance of the Centennial Building, local people formed the Waggoner Centennial Players. Every year, they put on the Centennial Players Dinner Theatre, and everybody pitches in. Actors decorate the tables and serve the food prior to their performance. Future Farmers of America kids wash the dishes. Performances sell out well in advance, and two hundred people each night crowd into the building for the nine performances and a steak dinner. The Centennial Players Dinner Theatre has been the glue that has held this community together long after the school and Main Street emptied.

TRAVELING THROUGH ILLINOIS

Many small towns also have an oft-told story about the time a celebrity passed through town. Waggoner is no exception. Waggoner was home to Bertha and Myron "Penny" Nail. At Penny's 100th birthday party, the whole town gathered for his celebration. His granddaughter, actress Kate Capshaw, came to the party and brought her husband, Steven Spielberg. Kate and Steven flew into Springfield and drove down I-55 for the festivities. In honor of Penny, they donated money to build Penny's Playground at the old school.

Descendants of the original Waggoners still live here, and Waggoner is still safe, slow-paced and brimming with small town pride and spirit. That's life in a small Illinois town.

64: Our Lady of the Highways

On the right stands a white Carrara marble statue of Mary, the mother of Jesus. The wooden and brick alcove around her and the cobblestone path that leads to her were assembled over fifty years ago by teens who lived in nearby towns. In 1959, the Litchfield Deanery's Catholic Youth Council chose to honor the Virgin Mary with a shrine that would be situated where all were welcome to visit. Young Loretta Marten asked her father if he would let them build it on his farm, which was adjacent to Route 66. (You can still see the original southbound lane of Route 66 directly in front of the statue.) Francis Marten agreed, and for his association with the shrine, he became one of five initial inductees into the Route 66 of Illinois Hall of Fame. Today, the next generation of the Marten family tends the beloved shrine.

Marlene Marten, Francis's daughter-in-law, said that visitors from all over the world stop at the shrine, most of them lured by the romance

Our Lady of the Highways. *LuAnn Cadden.*

of traveling Route 66 from Chicago to Los Angeles. She's met visitors from Europe, Australia and Great Britain. One day, as Marlene was gardening and up to her elbows in mud, an enthusiastic traveler asked if she could pose for a picture. Marlene laughed to think that somewhere in the world, some stranger has a picture of her in her gardening finest tucked in their photo album.

On October 25, 1959, three hundred people attended the ceremony to dedicate the statue that would become famous along Route 66. The $400 statue of Mary was imported from Italy, and lights were installed so travelers could view the shrine by day and night. Over the years, this little shrine has been visited by millions and was featured in numerous articles, books and television specials. On the fiftieth anniversary of its dedication, the Martens held a celebration mass on their farm. The Morton building was emptied of its machinery and converted into a church for the 150 attendees. Tractors and combines were moved out, and an altar was moved in. Wooden benches and hay bales served humbly as pews for the happy congregation. Loretta Marten and some of the other members from the Catholic Youth Council returned to honor the shrine they had worked so hard to place along this highway.

The Holy Mother was placed here to watch over travelers on what was once called the "Mother Road" by John Steinbeck. In his book *The Grapes of Wrath*, he wrote, "66 is the path of a people in flight, refugees from dust and shrinking land, from the thunder of tractors and shrinking ownership…From all of these the people are in flight, and they come into 66 from the tributary side roads…and the rutted country roads. 66 is the mother road, the road of flight."

You can take exit 63 to visit this shrine that has encouraged decades of pilgrims in their flight along both Route 66 and I-55.

60: Feeding the World

The Pioneer Hi-Bred Production Plant on the right receives special varieties of wheat and soybean seed from area farms. Here the seed is cleaned, packaged and shipped throughout the Midwest. Most seed comes from farms within a sixty-mile radius. Pioneer is the world's leading developer of genetically enhanced seeds used to increase farmer productivity here in Illinois and throughout the world. The U.S. Census Bureau estimates that the human population grows by more than 214,000 individuals each day. So, by this time tomorrow, there will be more than 200,000 more stomachs to fill, and next year, there will be another 78 million mouths to feed. While population increases, farmable land on this tiny planet does not. Pioneer reduces global hunger by making existing fields more productive. Pioneer distributes seeds of major crops like corn, soybeans, sorghum, rice and wheat, as well as other crops like sunflower, alfalfa, canola, millet and mustard. Like millions of other people, you probably have eaten food produced from Pioneer seeds.

59: From Coal Mines to Cornfields to Cows

Ahead on the left is Honey Bend Herefords. The Banovic family has owned this farmland since 1954, but they are a four-generation mining family. Over the years, they simultaneously worked in two of Illinois' biggest industries: coal mining and agriculture. The first year that the Banovics farmed here, they did not yet know what they were doing. They planted eighty acres of corn and beans and ended up weeding those entire fields by hand when not working at their day jobs in the mines and in Springfield. That summer, they lost their first corn crop to a drought. They almost decided that farming wasn't for them, but they persevered, harvested the poor corn crop and went into the hog business so that they could feed the small corncobs to pigs.

Their original house sat along Route 66 (under what is now the southbound lanes of I-55), but it was destroyed in 1970 when the interstate was built. Today, their five-hundred-acre operation on the right is run by Ed Banovic, a retired federal mine inspector. He took over the farm in the early 1980s when his father and mother moved to Washington, D.C., after his dad was elected secretary-treasurer of the United Mine Workers of America. Ed raises "polled" Herefords, genetically modified Herefords that don't grow horns. He switched to Herefords for two reasons. His dad told him that it costs the same to feed a valuable cow as it does an average cow. The other reason he switched from Angus to Herefords is that Herefords are notoriously gentle and docile and therefore safe around his grandchildren. Ed currently has thirty mother cows from which he sells embryos and calves to other breeders. Many men play golf or go fishing when they retire. Ed's retirement is devoted to creating superior cows.

SOUTHBOUND

56: Grain Trains and Coal Cars

At the next mile, the highway is raised over a railroad. Grain trains and coal cars pass under Interstate 55 and continuously move the outputs of Illinois' two largest industries from grain elevators and mining companies. Like a needle and thread, their steel pierces the soil and sews together lines from grain elevators to millers, coal mines to power plants. Since the late 1800s, trains carried crops, but the "unit train" didn't start rolling until the 1960s. A unit train is a railroad train that transports a single commodity from a single beginning point to a single destination. This allows a speedier transport than having to stop and pull out cars at different stops. Unit trains had previously been used for coal, but in 1967, the Cargill Company (mile 160) was the first company to run a unit train for grain. The 115-car Illinois Central train transported 400,000 bushels of corn to Baton Rouge, Louisiana.

Marc Johnson has hauled grain and coal along the railroad for twenty-five years. From his engineer's chair, he sits as high as if he were sitting in the hoop on a basketball court. He leaves his terminal with empty rail cars to begin his twelve-hour, one-hundred- to two-hundred-mile trip for the day. Traveling at fifty-five miles per hour, he pulls 110 to 115 rail cars in a six-thousand- to seven-thousand-foot line. Usually, he sits comfortably in an air-conditioned engine, but sometimes he and conductor Wade McClendon get an old 1960s model, where they must keep the windows open and endure the heat and unceasing noise. When the men pull up to their first grain elevator of the day, they leave their posts and take a break while the grain company spends between eight to sixteen hours loading the cars. Once loaded, they take their train to the next elevator and do the same and then return back to their terminal, where another crew takes the grain to a mill or port in its next step on the way to the market. When fully loaded, their train can weigh fifteen thousand tons.

Unfortunately, Illinois' train safety record is one of the worst in the country. In 2010, Illinois had the second-highest number of highway/rail grade crossing collisions in the country (125) and had the second-highest number of fatalities (27). By the time an engineer sees someone on the tracks, it is too late for the train to stop. It takes more than a mile to stop a train. Imagine putting on your breaks at mile 54, but not coming to a stop until you pass mile 53. The force of a freight train hitting an automobile is like your car running over a aluminum can.

Like postal carriers on rails, "Neither snow, nor rain, nor heat" stop the railroads from moving commerce. Marc has seen tracks raised five feet in a flood and debris from derailments moved off the tracks within a matter of hours. From moving everything from corn to coal, railroads keep the state's products rolling.

52: Planting the Prairie

It is amazing how many acres of farmland border Interstate 55. Now imagine how many hours of care go into managing that land. Today's farms are much larger than farms a century ago, but technology has helped make that possible. More than a century ago, farmers would often be seen guiding their plow or harrow with oxen or horse and planting by hand. It was a long, backbreaking process.

Settler C.G. Taylor described the planting of sod corn as "sticking an axe or spade between the layers of sod, and after dropping the corn, applying the heel of the boot freely." An account from the 1830s noted that farmers planted a whole handful of seeds in a clump, figuring, "One for the blackbird, and one for the crow, one for the cutworm, and two left to grow." The resulting field resembled an irregular assortment of clumps of cornstalks rather than the straight rows of corn we see today. No doubt that

Farmer in the late 1800s. *Sangamon Valley Collection, Lincoln Library.*

when Galesburg's George Brown invented a horse-drawn, two-row pull-type planter in 1851, subsequent planting must have been a little easier.

With even the smallest of today's tractors, farmers can plant ten acres per hour. Boot heels don't nearly take the wear and tear as the old days as they rest on the floor of an air-conditioned cab. While the farmer sits on his cushioned chair, GPS systems and computerized dashboards tell the planters exactly where to drop the seeds for the next row with the precision of a factory assembly line. Six- to twenty-four-row planters and harvesters do their work with incredible speed. Farmers' palms today are spared for other work, while herbicides kill off the weeds that would need pulling. Today's farmers manage the land with more steel than sweat, thereby increasing crop yields, decreasing labor costs and producing the abundant and inexpensive food we enjoy today.

48: Highway Huggers

The trees that hug the highway for the next few miles not only hold the soil tightly along the highway but also provide essential windbreaks, snow fences, shade, wildlife habitat and beautiful sculptural distractions from the level horizon. Architect Frank Lloyd Wright said, "The best friend of man is the tree. When we use the tree respectfully and economically, we have one of the greatest resources on the earth."

Paradoxically, trees produce lumber that is sometimes turned into roadside billboards that block your view of trees. Billboard laws on Interstate 55 are stringent enough that drivers can enjoy the view without an advertisement shielding them from the land. In 1971, the Illinois Highway Advertising Control Act began to regulate all signs, including billboards within 660 feet of interstate highways. Regulations keep billboards smaller than 1,200 square feet, prohibit distracting flashing lights and make sure that billboards don't line the entire highway's length like dominoes. Hopefully, no one will ever have to peak around billboards to enjoy a prairie sunset along this highway. "Song of the Open Road," Ogden Nash's 1933 parody of Joyce Kilmer's "Trees" poem, could have been penned for many other stretches of interstates, but thankfully not for this one:

> *I think that I shall never see*
> *A billboard lovely as a tree.*
> *Perhaps, unless the billboards fall,*
> *I'll never see a tree at all.*

TRAVELING THROUGH ILLINOIS

46: Mother Jones

Back at mile 64, you saw a monument to the most famous mother in history. Exit 44 takes you to the Union Miners Cemetery and a monument to another famous mother: "Mother" Mary Harris Jones. Mother Jones is buried in this cemetery along with eight miners who were shot while trying to stop a train of armed strikebreakers. In 1897, Chicago-Virden Coal Company miners went on strike for a forty-cent per ton of coal wage increase. On October 12, about sixty miners tried to stop a train of strikebreakers on their way to Virden. The eight miners who died that day became national heroes in the fight for laborer rights. In spite of the casualties, the strikers successfully diverted the strikebreakers, gained higher wages and furthered the cause of the newly formed United Mine Workers of America.

Mother Jones became a nationwide hero for laborers. She dedicated more than half her lifetime to fighting for their rights. She participated in strikes and supported laborers such as railroad workers in Alabama, streetcar workers in Texas and New York and female brewery bottlers in Milwaukee. She once said, "My address is like my shoes. It travels with me. I abide where there is a fight against wrong." Carl Sandburg's *The American Songbag* suggested that Mother Jones was the inspiration for the lyrics to the popular folk song, "She'll Be Comin' Round the Mountain," a hymnal of hope the miners sang as they awaited her arrival to help them ignite their labor unions.

Perhaps her empathy with the neglected working class began in Chicago when she was a seamstress for wealthy landowners along Lake Shore Drive. She saw the ragged jobless pass by the windows and said that her employers "seemed to neither notice nor care." After the 1871 Chicago Fire destroyed her house, her home became the road where she endlessly traveled to help laborers. This woman, who had lost her husband and all four children to yellow fever, became the "mother" of all who struggled to support their families through hard, fair work. When she died, Reverend John W.F. Maguire said, "Wealthy coal operators and capitalists throughout the United States are breathing sighs of relief while toil-worn men and women are weeping tears of bitter grief. The reason for this contrast of relief and sorrow is apparent. Mother Jones is dead."

Mary Harris Jones asked that she be buried alongside her eight brave boys:

> *When the last call comes for me to take my final rest, will the miners see that I get a resting place in the same clay that shelters the miners who gave up their lives of the hills of Virden, Illinois on the morning of October 12, 1897, for*

Southbound

their heroic sacrifice of their fellow men. They are responsible for Illinois being the best organized labor state in America. I hope it will be my consolation when I pass away to feel I sleep under the clay with those brave boys.

43: Pigeons

Around overpasses and farmsteads, you may see flocks of multicolored pigeons swirling in great arcs or gliding with silver wings upturned. In winter, you may see them sunning on the barn roofs. Woody Allen called them "winged rats." However, there is much to like about pigeons. Pigeons amuse city dwellers, who feed them from park benches, bringing to city folk what Roger Tory Peterson called "the most vivid expression of life." Pigeons have been clocked at speeds up to ninety-four miles per hour. Ancient Romans used pigeons to carry news back to Rome of Caesar's conquest of Gaul. Centuries later, news of Napoleon's defeat at Waterloo reached England by carrier pigeon four days ahead of the news carried by horse and ship.

The U.S. Army Signal Corps used fifty thousand pigeons to carry correspondences during World War II. About seventeen thousand pigeons were parachuted to supporters of the resistance in occupied Europe. In response, Hitler ordered all pigeons flying toward Britain to be shot down. Pigeons heroically delivered messages after having been shot or injured, some dying immediately after having delivered their message. One bird, Cher Ami, saved an entire U.S. battalion behind enemy lines, losing an eye and a leg in the process. Upon her return, medics fitted the pigeon with a wooden leg. They are not just war heroes. In medieval times, pigeons were raised for food, and their guano was used for fertilizer.

Today, pigeon as "breast of squab" still graces French menus. Pigeon racing is a thriving sport, particularly in Great Britain, where the Royal Pigeon Racing Association has forty-six thousand members. Even the queen has a pigeon loft! Pigeons with a good pedigree fetch tens of thousands of dollars. For millennia, pigeons have provided lifesaving communications, amusement, food and sport.

39: Madison County

This county is also famed as the hunting ground of the piasa bird. According to Indian legend, a frightening dragon-like creature hovered over this land, preying on humans and large animals. In 1675, French explorers Joliet and Marquette recorded seeing a painting of this creature on the bluffs near Alton. Marquette described the beastly painting as being "as large as a calf, with horns on the head like a deer, a fearful look, red eyes, bearded like a tiger, the face somewhat like a man's, the body covered with scales, and the tail so long that it twice makes a turn of the body, passing over the head and down between the legs, and ending at last, in a fish's tail."

The word *piasa* in Illini means "bird that devours men." In an uncanny link, another story relates how a similar bird carried off a boy in Lawndale. Read about it at mile 135N. Luckily, along I-55 today, the only large birds flying over your car in Madison County will be turkey vultures or an occasional bald eagle. Read more about the history of Madison County at 16N.

37: Seeing Pink and Saying "Cheese"

While the piasa bird may be myth, ahead on your right is a land of giants and colossal pink elephants, giant ice cream cones and gingerbread gazebos, spaceships and other-worldly possessions. These collectibles sit outside the Pink Elephant Antique Mall. Since 2005, this yard art has enticed interstate travelers to stop for a closer look. Owner Dave Hammond traveled all over the country to salvage these oddities and bring them home to the front yard of I-55. Why? Because he likes to see people smile. Hammond said that you wouldn't believe how many people over the years have stopped just to have their picture taken next to one of these objects. After he met several enthusiastic road-tripping photographers who stopped to take pictures of his first lawn creature, the pink elephant, he liked the idea of adding more and more, just for fun.

Getting these structures here wasn't always easy. When Hammond and his father traveled to Ohio to purchase the giant ice cream cone, they found it scattered in pieces in a snowy ditch and, fittingly, frozen to the ground. In eight-degree weather, they painstakingly freed it during a snowstorm that dropped ten inches of snow, making it an icy ride home for their ice cream cone. Hammond used a forklift to haul the twenty-six-foot-tall "Beach Guy" out of a densely wooded Wisconsin forest—a true Bigfoot. The Beach Guy originally held a Pepsi-Cola can and had a brief cameo in the 1990 film *Flatliners*. The gazebo was rolled in from Branson, Missouri, and the spaceship (read an entire story about it at mile 35N) was transported from Springfield, Illinois. The Muffler Man was moved in from Kentucky, and the half-elephants were hauled from Mills Mall in St. Louis. The thirteen-foot tricycle was pedaled in from just down the road, and as for the famous pink elephant, it has been on Route 66 for years. It just migrated a bit farther north from its spot at a Mexican restaurant in Granite City.

The antique mall's building dates back to 1949, when it was the Livingston High School. The old classrooms in the upstairs are now storage rooms, while the gymnasium floor is covered with antiques and collectibles. Wouldn't Hammond's lawn have been the perfect school playground?

32: St. Paul Lutheran Church

Ahead on the right, you can see the top of the St. Paul Lutheran Church's bell tower. Since 1931, this bell tower and façade have punctuated the prairie sky and comforted travelers along Route 66 and I-55. A German Lutheran community settled here in 1854 and built its first church where St. Paul's parking lot is today. When the church was dedicated on July 7, 1861, Pastor John Moll exclaimed, "The somewhat lonely and painfully monotonous prairie has now reason to rejoice."

St. Paul Lutheran, Church of the Neon Cross. *LuAnn Cadden.*

Traveling through Illinois

As the years passed, this site has been the gathering place for rejoicing in this community—a temple where people entered into baptism, became confirmed, received Communion, married their sweethearts and exited this world.

An electric cross on the front of the church glows in the evening and gives comfort to many travelers on I-55. At 30N, read more about how this cross came to be placed on the church and about its strong influence on those who drive the route.

28: Blackbirds

You may have noticed blackbirds on the fences and in vegetation along the highway, especially in wet roadside ditches with cattails. These are red-winged blackbirds, possibly the most abundant North American bird. Male red-wings use their red shoulder patches to defiantly defend territories and attract up to fifteen different mates to their roadside kingdoms. (In fact, in experiments for which their red patches were painted black, the male blackbirds lost their territories to other males they had previously defeated.) During nesting season, male red-winged blackbirds may attack much larger birds like hawks and crows. If you happen to notice a big bird being chased by a smaller bird, you are witnessing this midair avian conflict.

The males return in the spring well before the females. Females, colored to blend in while sitting on the nest, are brown with streaked breasts. As you speed past in spring and summer, you might notice a male red-wing flashing its red epaulets, throwing its head back and letting loose with its emphatic song. The male red-wing's song is a symbol of spring's arrival and part of the soundtrack of summer along Illinois roadsides.

During winter, blackbirds form large, noisy flocks that sometimes number in the millions of birds. Some observers have reported that they felt the warmth of the birds' collective bodies when such a flock flew near. Nineteenth-century naturalist-philosopher Henry David Thoreau wrote eloquently about the impression such blackbird flocks made on him: "[S]ome rising, others falling, yet all advancing together, one flock but many birds, some silent, some tchucking—incessant alternation. This harmonious movement as in a dance, this agreeing to differ, makes charm of the spectacle to me." During winter months, watch for such impressive animated blackbird flocks flying over the fields and farms along the highway.

25: Barn Billboards

Ahead, just after mile 24 on the right, you will see a barn used as an advertisement for Meramec Caverns, a popular tourist attraction in Stanton, Missouri. In the early 1930s, Lester B. Dill, the Meramec Caverns owner, noticed signs in Florida painted on barns encouraging travelers to "See Rock City" or "Chew Mail Pouch Tobacco." He decided to try that for his caverns. During the heyday of barn advertisements in the 1950s, more than three hundred barns in twenty-six states, including as far away as California, had signs for Meramec Caverns. Originally, in return for allowing the Meramec Caverns sign to be painted on their barn, the owner was given a railroad pocket watch, the wife was given a box of chocolates, the family was given a free pass into Meramec Caverns and, most importantly, the entire barn received a fresh coat of paint. Roadside beautification laws prevent new ads from being painted, but preservation groups have restored original advertisements. Hobbyists from over the United States seek out and photograph the few remaining advertising barns. Mr. Dill also is credited with inventing the bumper sticker. He tied cardboard "bumper signs" on visitors' bumpers in the caverns parking lot. Soon he began experimenting with different adhesives. Early versions had wax paper backing that would be peeled off to expose flypaper-like glue. In the 1960s, politicians made bumper stickers commonplace and created bad feelings by using glue that made them difficult to remove.

23: Landlocked Sailors

Exit 23 takes you to either Edwardsville or Marine. Edwardsville is named for Ninian Edwards, the governor of Illinois Territory at the time this town was established in 1812. You can read about Edwardsville at 22N. But Marine? How did a midwestern town, about as distant as you can get from an ocean in either direction, get that name? When a group of New England sea captains, led by Curtis Blakeman and George Allen, chose to retire here in the middle of the country, local residents named the area the Marine Settlement. Although no sea salt flavors the prairie air, perhaps the men did enjoy the constant motion of the ocean of prairie grasses rolling and crashing in windy waves to the distant horizon.

Traveling through Illinois

22: Paul Simon Freeway

The bow tie on the sign on the right immediately calls to mind one particular Illinois politician: Paul Simon. In 2006, this stretch of highway was dedicated as the Paul Simon Freeway in honor of the bow tie–wearing Democratic senator. Simon came to Illinois from Oregon at the age of nineteen to help a struggling newspaper. He not only saved the *Troy Tribune* but also built a chain of thirteen newspapers and became the youngest newspaper publisher in the United States. Between 1984 and 1997, he served as a U.S. senator who truly sought the opinion of his constituents. He held more than six hundred town meetings throughout the state—more than any senator in the state's history. On the day this sign was unveiled, Lieutenant Governor Pat Quinn said, "Senator Paul Simon's integrity and intelligence inspired everyone who knew him. I hope everyone who drives on this new Paul Simon Parkway and Freeway will be reminded of Senator Simon's tireless advocacy for the rights of everyday people."

21: From Rail to Trail

Just ahead, hikers and bicyclists cross above semi-trucks on a trailway that was once part of the Illinois Central Railway, one of three railroads that served Glen Carbon. In 1892, an English businessman in the coal industry named the village Carbon Glen, meaning Coal Valley. His daughter convinced him that Glen Carbon sounded better. Today, rubber bike tires roll quietly along the path where steel wheels used to scream. The other two railroad lines that served Glen Carbon also have been converted to trails, thereby creating a branching network of more than eighty-five miles of trailway along the original lines that once stimulated local growth and prosperity. Walkers and riders can travel through tunnels and across timber trestle bridges, past prairies of swaying grasses and over bluffs above winding waterways on the Glen Carbon Trail.

17: Mile-by-Mile Marker

Just ahead, Interstate 55 travelers drive part of the Historic National Road called Route 40, the nation's first federally funded interstate. Mile 17 is the exit for Route 40 east. From there, you can follow this famous road from here to East St. Louis and then west toward its terminus in Utah.

Southbound

More than two hundred years ago, travelers on this, the nation's first interstate, used mile markers just as you are using today. Back in 1811, mile markers made of stone guided coach drivers and horseback riders every five miles along the trail. In 1835, new cast-iron obelisk mile markers replaced the stone. Today, some stone mile markers can still be found along the old trail that is known as "the road that built the nation." Read more about this Historic National Road at 14N.

Early mile markers also lined a trail that long preceded I-55, according to an 1882 history of Madison County. It noted that "county authorities laid out and opened a road from Edwardsville to Clear Lake on the Sangamon, a distance of seventy miles, as early as 1820, surveyed by Jacob Judy, who caused mile posts to be erected along the entire length of the said road, which is known to our readers as the 'Springfield' road."

12: Can You See It Yet?

This is often the question that children and inquisitive adults persistently ask when approaching St. Louis. Passengers anxiously scan the sky for the tallest manmade monument in the nation: the silver Gateway Arch on the grounds of the Jefferson National Expansion Memorial in St. Louis. You can inform your anxious passengers that at the next mile (11.2), they will get their first glimpse of the silver rainbow. Imagine the southbound Interstate 55 travelers who see, for the first time, this 886-ton stainless steel structure rising 630 feet over the Mississippi River, twice as high as the Statue of Liberty and arching gracefully over the horizon. You might not have to imagine if you *are* one of those first-timers today. What a thrill to see a gateway of exploration, welcoming you to the West. After crossing the Mississippi River, you could be one of the millions of visitors each year who take elevators to the top for a 360-degree, thirty-mile view.

10: Cahokia Mounds

It may be hard to imagine, but as you drive between miles 10 and 6, you are passing through what was once the northern border of one of the biggest cities in the world. In AD 1250, Cahokia was the largest prehistoric native civilization, and it is the largest archaeological site north of Mexico. At its peak, it was comparable to the size of nearby Collinsville, covered about six

TRAVELING THROUGH ILLINOIS

Community Life at Cahokia, by Michael Hampshire. I-55 is directly behind the large Monks Mound. *Cahokia Mounds State Historic Site.*

square miles and had a population of twenty thousand people. Ruled by a chief and an elite class, the city was laid out neatly, with houses in rows and agricultural fields on the outskirts of town.

Between AD 700 and AD 1400, more than 120 earthen mounds were built, some as pedestals for the homes of prominent citizens, some as burial mounds and one particularly impressive mound to elevate the chief's home. I-55 construction partially covered some of these grassy mounds. Between the row of trees on your left (between 8.6 and 8.2), you'll see Monks Mound, the largest man-made earthen mound in North America. The chief lived on top of this hill, and apparently, it was the site of human sacrifices to honor him and their bountiful corn crop. It took three hundred years to build the one-hundred-foot-tall mound, whose fourteen-acre base is larger than that of the Great Pyramid of Giza.

What happened to this thriving civilization is a mystery. The population dwindled and disappeared. Other tribes could not tell Europeans much about this civilization when the explorers first saw the impressive mounds. You can take exit 10 or 6 to climb to the top of Monks Mound for an incredible view of St. Louis or to visit the Cahokia Mounds Visitor Center to learn more about this mysterious and impressive civilization.

7: Wetlands, Not Wastelands

The marsh on your right is a remnant of the habitat that existed with the Cahokians—the bottomlands of the Mississippi. Some wetlands are cattail marshes like this one, whereas other wetlands are wooded swamps or moist meadows. However, all wetlands, regardless of type and size, are valuable. Wetlands can clean pollutants from water, add to groundwater supplies, prevent costly flooding, stabilize banks, reduce erosion, provide homes for wildlife and create opportunities for birding, canoeing, hunting or just enjoying the miracles and music of nature. Until recently, people considered wetlands a nuisance and drained them, mostly to convert them to cropland. More than 90 percent of the wetlands that existed in Illinois at the time of European settlement have been destroyed. The remaining wetlands are critical to Illinois plants and animals.

The cumulative effects of wetlands are significant. Wetlands, large or small, are not wastelands; they are wonderful resources that give beautiful and useful gifts to society. Read more at 4N about the animals that rely on the wetland habitat as their home.

6: Wasteland Mound

The twenty-story-tall hill on the right dwarfs the nearby Cahokia Indian mounds. This modern mound is Waste Management's Milam Landfill. Garbage is brought to this 176-acre landfill from as far away as Ohio, Iowa and Kansas. It has reached its capacity and is expected to close in 2013. Local residents are concerned about this closing as the taxes from this landfill contribute $1.5 million per year to the village of Fairmont City, half of the city's operating budget.

5: Meet Me in St. Louis

At mile 5.4, the silver Gateway Arch beckons to travelers as they near the Mississippi River, which created and nourishes the surrounding wetlands. For centuries, these wetlands were known as the American Bottom. In the 1800s, travelers wrote of the natural confluences of water, forest and prairie in the American Bottom. Some recorded their distaste for the marshy area.

Others recorded the beauty of the "wide prairie [that] stretches for miles its carpeting of green, gemmed with the most beautiful flowers, and dotted, at intervals, with clusters of trees." It was a "sea of verdure, spangled with the brightest flowers."

Over the next few miles, a tangle of interstates and ramps deliver you to the Mississippi River and a confluence of four great national highways. Travelers from Colorado's I-70, Chesapeake's I-64, Wichita Falls' I-44 and New

Traveling through Illinois

A view of the St. Louis skyline from Monks Mound. *LuAnn Cadden.*

Orleans' I-55 all converge here on their journeys across the nation. Three great rivers—the Missouri, Mississippi and Illinois—also converge near here, bringing with them waters from Montana mountains, Minnesota lakes and Illinois prairies. The convergence of these highways and waterways forms a great crossroads of the nation.

A Fond Farewell

As Illinois meets Missouri over the center of the Mighty Mississippi, this crossroad comes alive as cars stream by, barges float below and airplanes cruise above. In Mark Twain's *Life on the Mississippi*, he described his beloved boyhood river by saying, "The face of the water, in time, became a wonderful book—a book that was a dead language to the uneducated passenger, but which told its mind to me without reserve, delivering its most cherished secrets as clearly as if it uttered them with a voice. And it was not a book to be read once and thrown aside, for it had a new story to tell every day."

We hope that you have enjoyed your drive along Interstate 55 and that with each journey you take across it, the road will open like a familiar yet new book, sharing its stories of past and present.

Part III
NORTHBOUND

WELCOME TO ILLINOIS

As Missouri and Illinois meet over the Mississippi River, highways and waterways meet to form the crossroads of our nation. This area is famous as the confluence of three great rivers and four great highways. Waters from Montana mountains, Minnesota lakes and Illinois prairies mix as the Missouri, Mississippi and Illinois Rivers become one. Here, Interstates 44, 55, 64 and 70 cross on their journeys across the nation. Over the next few miles, concrete is the prevailing land feature, but for centuries, marshes and swamps dominated the area.

In the 1800s, travelers wrote of the natural mingling of water, forest and prairie in this area they called American Bottom. Some recorded their distaste for the area, which was "often marshy and abounding in stagnant lagoons and backwaters, which are filled, when the river overflows its banks...and on the subsidence of waters, are left full of vegetable matter to putrify in an almost tropical sun." Others recorded their awe of the beautiful flower-filled prairie. Today, roadways cover the old wetland areas, but some remnants, such as the one ahead, still remain.

Traveling through Illinois

From St. Louis to Chicago

4: At Home on a Wetland

The marsh on your right is a remnant of the Mississippi's reach. Some wetlands are wooded swamps, while others are moist meadows. Some are farmed and grazed, and some are merely roadside ditches. However, all wetlands teem with a diversity of life. About half of the ninety-five threatened or endangered animals in Illinois use wetlands. In fact, although wetlands make up only about 5 percent of land in the United States, 31 percent of all plants in the country are wetland plants. If you look closely and quickly, you might see blackbirds, wood ducks, the four-foot-tall great blue herons or white egrets wading between muskrat mounds.

As you continue along I-55, you will notice other, smaller wetlands. Read more at 7S about how wetlands are useful habitats for humans, too.

6: Cahokia Mounds

As you drive between miles 6 and 10, you are passing through what was once the northern border of the Cahokia civilization. In AD 1250,

Interstate 55 (shown near mile 7) slices through Cahokia, seen just on the other side of the trees. *Cahokia Mounds State Historic Site.*

Northbound

An aerial perspective of Cahokia circa AD 1150–1200, by William R. Iseminger. I-55 runs where the creek on the north was located. *Cahokia Mounds State Historic Site.*

Cahokia was the largest prehistoric native civilization in the world. At its peak, it was comparable to the size of nearby Collinsville, covered nearly six square miles, and had a population of twenty thousand people. Today, visitors can get guided interpretive tours in the park-like setting of grassy mounds, climb to the top of the Cahokia ruler's largest mound—Monk's Mound—and learn about the Cahokia people in the Cahokia Visitor Center.

Behind the row of trees, directly to the right of mile 8, is Monk's Mound, the largest man-made earthen mound in North America. (Look back over your shoulder at mile 8.2 to see it.) Read more about Monk's Mound and the Cahokia civilization at 10S.

Underneath your tires, artifacts of the Cahokia people probably still remain. Just ahead, beneath the interchange of I-255, I-55 and I-70, archaeologists found the "Birger figure," a statue of a woman wielding a short-handled Mississippian stone hoe. She's chopping earth that resembles the back of a snake, and she has the head of a cat and a tail that turns into a squash vine climbing up the woman's back. Cahokia was laid out neatly, with houses in rows and agricultural fields on the outskirts of town.

9: Cahokia Corn

Drivers heading north on I-55 notice that Illinois' original prairie grasses and wildflowers have been mostly replaced by cornfields. But corn is not new to Illinois. In fact, one thousand years ago, Cahokia's cornstalks sprouted right here, just as they do in the field to the right of you. The Cahokia people were mainly an agricultural group who surrounded their city with crop fields. As you drive between miles 9 and 12, you would be slicing right through what one thousand years ago would have been cornfields on the northeastern edge of their village. Corn production helped the Cahokia civilization prosper and rise to its peak population of twenty thousand people.

Europeans did not know that corn existed until Columbus brought some back from Cuba in 1492. Native Americans first acquired food by hunting and gathering. More than four thousand years ago, Native Americans began planting crops such as squash and sunflowers. Then, between one thousand and two thousand years ago, as corn cultivation spread north from Mexico, Indians began planting corn throughout the current United States. They grew corn with blue, red, black and yellow kernels. The sweet corn that we eat directly off the cob was not developed until the 1700s.

11: No Bluffing

The bluffs you're climbing right here mark the boundary of the previously mentioned American Bottom floodplain. Over thousands of years, the Mississippi River's channels fluctuated drastically in their wide, weaving, braiding arteries that ebbed, flowed and eventually dried into rich soil. The lifeblood of this region, now tamed into one navigable channel, has left behind oxbow lakes, ponds, streams, smoothed bottomland and cradling bluffs.

12: Where in the World Are You?

Within the next mile, you will cross the ninetieth meridian west. Meridians are straight lines used on maps and in navigation that extend from the North Pole to the South Pole. So, what does crossing the ninetieth meridian mean to you? Well, it means that right now you are precisely due north of Memphis, New Orleans, the Yucatan Peninsula and the Galapagos Islands—all places along this meridian. It also means that you are a quarter of the way around the world from the Royal Observatory in Greenwich, England, a suburb of London, which establishes the Prime Meridian's (zero degrees of longitude) location. This means that you are on the exact opposite side of the planet from ninetieth meridian east, which passes through Russia, Mongolia, China and Bangladesh. It also means that you are at the exact center of the Central Time Zone. Clocks here are in sync with the sun overhead. When the sun is directly above the ninetieth meridian, it is noon Central Standard Time.

14: The Road that Built the Nation

From East St. Louis to Troy, just ahead, I-55 travelers drive a part of the Historic National Road, the first federally funded interstate in the nation. In 1806, the same year Lewis and Clark returned from their exploration of the newly acquired Louisiana Purchase, President Thomas Jefferson proposed a federal highway that would cut through the Allegheny Mountains and transport goods and people to the west. In 1811, work started on this eight-hundred-mile route that would encourage commerce and settlement from Baltimore to the Mississippi River. Work continued to Vandalia, Illinois, until 1838, when they ran out of money for the project. By 1843, Illinois citizens had extended the highway to Troy and, later, all the way to San Francisco as U.S. Route 40. Route 40 continued to carry explorers west, via automobiles rather than covered wagons. During its heyday from the 1920s to the 1960s, the road became a highway for vacationers who could stop and marvel at spectacles like the world's largest catsup bottle. In 1949, the 170-foot-tall Brooks Catsup bottle became a dual water tower and advertisement just south of Collinsville's downtown. Renovations and the National Register of Historic Places recognition in 2002 have kept its shelf life fresh for today's travelers to still relish.

16: Madison County

They came from Ohio, Kentucky, Massachusetts, Georgia, Tennessee and the Carolinas, lured by tales of fertile lands at the confluence of the Mississippi, Missouri and Illinois Rivers. They raised corn, cotton, castor beans, wheat and hogs. When early settlers formed Madison County in 1812, it expanded over half the state, covering the entire route of I-55 from

St. Louis to Chicago. As new counties formed, it was reduced to its current size by 1848. An early settler here said that the necessaries of life in the new Illinois territory were "hog and hominy." The pioneers farmed the fertile soil and introduced apple and other fruit trees. By the late 1800s, the county also had become an industrial area of steel and oil and was famous as the home of Graniteware—the metal cookware that's been used around the campfire since the 1800s.

This county is also famed as the hunting ground of the piasa bird, a human-devouring dragon-like creature. Read more about the frightening piasa bird at 39S. In an uncanny link, another story relates how a similar bird carried off a boy in Lawndale. Read about it ahead at mile 135N.

18: What's that Cargo?

To your left, trucks sit, rather than roll, along the highway. Truck Centers Inc. is a family-owned business that provides truck drivers with new and used trucks, vehicle parts, a twenty-four-hour full service and even a shower, snacks and television while they wait. Most travelers disregard the many trucks that they pass on the highway. But these trucks, designed to haul a wide variety of products, deserve a closer look. The "box" trailer is the most common truck you will see and will haul anything that will fit in its rectangular frame. The "reefer" is even cooler—a box trailer with a cooling unit to keep dairy products cold and produce fresh. A "tanker" hauls liquids like gasoline, whereas a "dry bulk" hauls dry materials like flour and sugar. "Flatbeds" may haul stacks of wood and other items that must be strapped down, while the "lowboy" is a flatbed that doesn't stack but rather can be lowered down to take in vehicles such as bulldozers, cranes and other heavy equipment. So, notice the diversity of these big rigs as they cruise down the highway and play a travel game of "What's that Cargo?"

19: Ag Country

You are now leaving the urban area and entering a sea of rich productive cropland. Over the next two hundred miles, you will pass many of Illinois' seventy-six thousand farms. Illinois farms cover more than 28 million acres—nearly 80 percent of the state's land. Illinois is a leading producer of corn, soybeans and hogs. Farmers here also raise other commodities, including cattle, wheat, sheep, poultry and specialty products such as alfalfa, horseradish, Christmas trees and even emus and ostriches. Illinois ranks second nationally in the export of agricultural products. Illinois farmers help feed the world with more than 44 percent of grain produced in Illinois exported. As you drive past mile after mile of lush croplands, consider how fortunate we are to have land that produces such bountiful harvests—harvests that we share with hungry people around the world.

21: From Rail to Trail

Just ahead, you will pass under the Glen Carbon Trail. The old Illinois Central overpass now is part of a Rails-to-Trails program that provides recreation corridors for communities. Where trains used to link towns, now these bikeways and walkways create a quieter slower-paced route. Read more about Glen Carbon at 21S.

22: Edwards Trace/Edwardsville

Another trail that brought commerce and growth to central Illinois was the Edwards Trace. Beginning in Kaskaskia, it passed through Edwardsville and headed north through Springfield, Elkhart and up to Peoria. Before 1830, this dirt path was the most direct land route from southern to northern Illinois. Edwardsville and the Edwards Trace were both named after Ninian Edwards, the governor of the Illinois Territory when the town was founded in 1812. During the War of 1812, he led an army along this path from Fort Russell (near present-day Edwardsville) to Fort Clark (Peoria).

But the roots of this trail go back even farther. Research suggests that prehistoric people and large mammals created this path in their seasonal journeys north and south. Other artifacts and data conclude that Illinois' Indian tribes traveled this road. Europeans also began using this path in the eighteenth century when French priests used it to travel from Cahokia to Lake Peoria. While the Mississippi and Illinois Rivers were the water routes for early missionaries, explorers and pioneers, the Edwards Trace was their land route. This trail led pioneers into the beautiful Sangamon Valley, where the capital city of Springfield began to grow. Traffic along I-55's dusty predecessor really began to pick up after Illinois became a state in 1818. In that same year, one early settler traveling north to Springfield described the trail through the

Traveling through Illinois

A depression in the land reveals the Edwards Trace at Lake Park in Springfield. *LuAnn Cadden.*

wilderness. "No house after we left Edwardsville, and nothing but an old Indian trail, and but one woman in all that region; but a fine country this was."

Over the years, other roads replaced the trail, and as more people moved in to farm the prairie, the trail became either farmland or a weed-covered depression on the landscape. But the soles of moccasins, boots and hooves, along with wagon wheels, had pressed a distinct path into the earth as they passed back and forth between the north and south. For years, this indentation was overlooked, until a historian unraveled the mystery of the path, which measures nearly two feet deep and six feet wide at its base. Part of Edwards Trace can still be seen today along Lake Springfield in Lake Park. Historical societies and the City of Springfield placed a marker recognizing the Edwards Trace so that this historic highway will never be forgotten.

25: Red Barns

Over the next few miles, you'll see red barns. We often think of barns as being red, but why that color? Some believe that farmers merely chose that color to provide sharp contrast with the green landscape. But a more accurate explanation may be that for many years the ingredients for red paint were cheap and easy to mix on the farm. Ready-to-use paint makes it easy for farmers to choose any color of paint for barns. But even with all the choices out there, you don't often see a purple or turquoise barn along the side of the road. You'll notice that many farmers still enjoy using the traditional red of the old farm. You will see several more red barns in the next twenty-five miles on I-55.

27: Green Thumbs for Blue Stars

At the rest stop ahead, a Blue Star Memorial Highway Marker honors the men and women who serve in the armed forces. At least forty-four such markers are placed throughout Illinois, and hundreds more reside along highways throughout the United States. In 1944, a New Jersey garden club planted eight thousand dogwood trees in tribute to the soldiers of World War II and designated that highway the Blue Star Drive. The blue star was chosen as the signature emblem since it was displayed on flags and the homes of families who had a son or daughter in the service.

The National Council of State Garden Clubs decided to spread this idea nationwide. It believed that with this national campaign, it could "beautify and preserve the country the men had fought for" with colorful living peaceful settings rather than build stone monuments that sat cold on a lawn. The program has grown to include all men and women in service. Three types of blue star markers can be found: the Memorial Highway Marker, found alongside roadways and at rest stops; the Blue Star Memorial Marker, found at veterans' hospitals and national cemeteries; and the Blue Star By-Way Marker, placed in garden settings. More than seventy thousand miles of highway are designated as Blue Star Memorial Highways, living greenways that will bloom anew each year and soldier on through our wars past, present and future.

30: Church of the Neon Cross

The cemetery ahead on the left contains tombstones from the 1800s up until the present day and records the lives of generations of St. Paul Lutheran Church's congregation. The church is up ahead near mile 31. Between the church and cemetery sits the remains of a dairy farm. Church services were scheduled around the hours of the dairy farm so members could balance their work with their worship.

Since 1931, St. Paul Lutheran Church's bell tower and façade have punctuated the prairie sky and comforted travelers along Route 66 and later I-55 with a neon blue cross that glows brilliantly every evening. The neon cross was placed on its façade in the 1940s. When church member Oscar Brunnworth was killed in World War II, his family raised this lighted blue neon cross in his memory. Travelers have written letters to the church expressing their appreciation for the comfort provided by this landmark. Truck drivers use the cross as a marker during their late-night journeys and count on seeing it when they pass this way. They have even called the church office to let them know when it has gone out so that the next time they pass by, it will be there to greet them.

32: Breaking the Prairie

Even though you have been driving past fields of corn and soybeans, it is unlikely that you've seen a farmer out walking among his crops. More than a century ago, farmers would often be seen guiding their plow or harrow (a spiked board use to break up soil into fine particles) with oxen or horse, planting by hand, cutting weeds and picking off pests. Granted, the acres they farmed were small in comparison to today's massive fields. But today's farmers don't suffer the same sunburn and physical labor.

NORTHBOUND

When Illinois' first farmers pierced the tough but fertile Illinois sod, they didn't merely plow; they had to "break the prairie." In 1856, settler C.G. Taylor wrote:

> *Many farmers use the heavy breaking plough, cutting a furrow from eighteen to twenty-six inches wide, and about three inches deep, requiring a force of from three to six yoke of oxen: of late, however, so many improvements have been made in the form and draught of ploughs, that the prairie can be readily broken, at the rate of one and a quarter to one and a half acres per day, with a single pair of horses.*

Today's farmers have other concerns about soil management now that the prairie has been broken. Pioneers found the soil naturally fertile, but this soil has been used many times since the first plows broke the prairie. Farmers rotate crops and add nutrients to their land in order to maintain adequate soil fertility. Their crop yields are higher and travel much farther than those that were harvested by their great-great-grandparents.

35: Out of This World!

In the past, farmers were seen working their plows in the fields; in the present, you see combines working miles of neat crop rows; and in the future, just ahead, you'll see...a flying saucer? Ahead, on your left, a UFO sits on the lawn of the Pink Elephant Antique Mall. Actually, it is an old model of the House of the Future (Futuro House). The antique mall's owner, Dave Hammond, added it to his collection of oddities that dot the lawn to give travelers something to talk about (read more about Hammond's mall at 37S).

This is just one of ninety-six Futuro Houses that have landed across the earth since the 1960s. Only nineteen made it to the United States. Manufactured in Finland, they were designed to be ski cabins. They were made completely from a lightweight plastic so that they could be assembled and disassembled with ease in a variety of places and climates—almost a kind of nomadic house or a mobile home without wheels. And in their moment of UFO glory, they actually flew over cities and to the tops of mountains, lifted by helicopters that helped them hover over their landing spot until they could be grounded as dwellings for skiers and homeowners. The House of the Future didn't prosper due to the 1970s oil crisis, which raised the price

Traveling through Illinois

The Futuro House at Pink Elephant Antique Mall. *LuAnn Cadden.*

of plastics too high for profitable production. But today, about sixty of these past-futuristic homes are still out there…somewhere.

This Futuro House was modeled at the Illinois State Fair in the late '60s and early '70s. Then, for almost three decades, it sat on private property along Illinois 29, just outside of Springfield, before Mr. Hammond purchased it and transported it here. He thought that it would make a great addition to his other quirky yard art. Hammond has cleaned up the nostalgic saucer and plans to turn it into a dining area for those curious travelers who stop by for an ice cream, lunch or antique shopping. But good luck explaining your highway stop to skeptical friends—you purchased your lunch from a giant ice cream cone and then ate it in a flying saucer, not to mention seeing the pink elephant near the parking lot.

38: Get Your Hits on Route 66

Along the frontage road on your left, you'll see a sign for Old Route 66, the legendary road that went from Chicago to Los Angeles. Route 66 festivals, museums, parades and memorabilia live on by the support of citizens and preservation groups. Along your I-55 drive, we'll often mention this well-loved highway as it relates to modern-day sights. But families, honeymooners and road wanderers weren't the only ones who enjoyed cruising the Illinois stretch of 66. Big-city gangsters and bootleggers ran this road between St. Louis and Chicago.

Just ahead, the town of Benld has stories about these Prohibition-era rumrunners of Route 66. In March 1928, the local paper recorded that Captain W.B. Murray of Chicago seized "one of the most complete and expensively constructed establishments for making illicit liquor" just one mile east of Benld. The huge distillery was sandwiched between coal mines named "Number 1" up through "Number 4." The secret distillery became mine "Number 5." It had three fifty-foot-high smokestacks and two fifty-thousand-gallon vats that contained thousands of gallons of alcohol awaiting shipment throughout central Illinois. Locals said that the bootlegging boss in Macoupin County (you'll enter it at mile 39) was Dominic Tarro, a Benld resident and owner of the Coliseum Ballroom on Route 66. In 1924, it was touted as the largest dance joint between St. Louis and Chicago. Greats such as Benny Goodman and Tommy Dorsey played in the ten-thousand-square-foot ballroom and entertained more than two thousand guests at a time, including Al Capone. In 1929, Tarro's car was found burned and riddled with bullet holes. Months later, his body, wrists and ankles bound with wire, was found in the Sangamon River. Tarro's ghost, among others, was said to frequent his old ballroom. Sadly, fire destroyed the Coliseum in 2011, evicting the spirits of guys and gals who enjoyed other "spirits" at the Coliseum and from old "Number 5."

43: Benld

Benld is one of many Illinois towns that grew from a coal mine. Coal mines encircled the town and lured European immigrants to settle and work here. This town was once a multilingual international village that included residents from Italy, Germany, Ireland, Lithuania, Greece, Croatia, Sweden, Scotland, Bohemia and Austria. Many towns are also named for their founder, as is this one, but this story may have a twist. The town was certainly named after founder Benjamin L. Dorsey, but legend here has it that the painter of the new town's sign fell when he got to the "d." It may just be legend, but it makes for a funny story.

TRAVELING THROUGH ILLINOIS

44: Mother Jones

Exit 44 takes you to the Union Miners Cemetery and a monument to "Mother" Mary Harris Jones. Mother Jones was a hero for laborers. Her fiery determination to improve human rights helped thousands of workers. She participated in strikes and supported laborers such as streetcar workers in Texas and New York, Colorado coal miners and female brewery bottlers in Milwaukee. When she died, Reverend John W.F. Maguire said, "Wealthy coal operators and capitalists throughout the United States are breathing sighs of relief while toil-worn men and women are weeping tears of bitter grief. The reason for this contrast of relief and sorrow is apparent. Mother Jones is dead." Mother Jones asked that she be buried here next to a group of men that died trying to stop a train of strikebreakers. Read more about her at 46S.

45: The Need for Trees

Enjoy the embracing tree-lined highway in this area, for the highway won't be hugged by trees during most of your drive toward Chicago. More often, you'll see trees lining fields, surrounding a farmhouse or dotted in huge agricultural fields. These trees on the vast, empty plains provide windbreaks, snow fences, shade, energy savings, erosion control, wildlife habitats and beautiful sculptural distractions from the level horizon. Many trees along this highway are well-respected elders—the survivors of tornadoes, drought, hail and heavy rains that have whipped around their lonely trunks, unprotected by a forest of others. Author Hermann Hesse admired the tree's life in human terms:

> *All it has experienced, tasted, suffered:*
> *The course of years, generations of animals,*
> *Oppression, recovery, friendship of sun and Wind*
> *Will pour forth each day in the song*
> *Of its rustling foliage, in the friendly*
> *Gesture of its gently swaying crown,*
> *In the delicate sweet scent of resinous*
> *Sap moistening the sleep-glued buds,*
> *And the eternal game of lights and*
> *Shadows it plays with itself, content.*

Northbound

As you travel farther north, we'll point out ways that trees can give us what we need along Interstate 55.

47: Kilroy Was on I-55

Just before mile 48, a rusty "Kilroy Was Here" sign hangs on the fence to the right. Kilroy has been "seen" all around the world, even though he remains one of the most mysterious characters of all time. Sightings of him have been reported at the Statue of Liberty, on top of Mount Everest, under the Arc de Triomphe and even on the moon. But who was (or is) this Kilroy, and why was he traveling I-55?

Many legends exist about Kilroy, but one logical story keeps reappearing. During World War II, ships were built quickly for the troops. James Kilroy was a ship inspector in Boston. If he had inspected the ship, and no one was there to sign off on it, he simply wrote, "Kilroy was here" on the bulkheads and moved on to inspect his next ship. In the haste of releasing the ships, some surfaces missed getting a final coat of paint, and when

Kilroy was here! *Lillian Cadden.*

soldiers would see the mysterious message, the stories and jokes began. The imaginative GIs began leaving "Kilroy" messages everywhere around the world for their comrades. Kilroy was found on a Japanese beach when GIs landed, on enemy equipment and on an outhouse constructed exclusively for the Potsdam conference attended by Truman, Stalin and Churchill. Supposedly, after Stalin stepped from the outhouse, he asked his aide, "Who is Kilroy?" Even Hitler wanted to know who Kilroy was—an Allied spy or perhaps a codename for some top-secret plan? More recently, Kilroy has been seen in Iraq and Afghanistan. We may never know why Kilroy was traveling I-55, but we do know that he is a friend of the American soldier, and we know that his hopeful and fun-loving spirit still travels the world.

51: Montgomery County

This county is named after Revolutionary War hero Richard Montgomery. He was born in Ireland and served as a captain in the British army before settling in New York. He became a courageous officer in the Continental army and led troops who captured Montreal from the British, but later he was killed attempting to conquer the city of Quebec on December 31, 1775. Montgomery's heroism was still fresh in the minds of Americans when town and counties were being settled and named. At least seventeen states in the eastern United States have a county named Montgomery, and countless towns are named for this American hero. Some early settlers here were soldiers from the War of 1812 who received 160 acres of "Soldiers' Bounty Lands" in the Illinois Territory. It was an award from Congress, but it was also an incentive to populate the western lands.

52: Moving Water

The stacks of green and blue pipes lying on the ground directly off to the right are the inventory of the North American Pipe Company. This firm is in the business of moving water to benefit people. It makes PVC pipes in sizes ranging from half an inch to thirty-six inches in diameter, servicing the city and rural water systems, sewer, plumbing, irrigation and do-it-yourself markets. This particular plant makes pipe up to eighteen inches in diameter. It produces more than 12 million pounds of pipe per year. Interestingly, pipe production is measured in pounds, but sales are measured in feet of pipe. Pipe from Litchfield is used all over the world to get water to new neighborhoods, move dirty water to be treated, bring water to thirsty crops and connect rural families to reliable city water systems.

55: Worldwide Weather Station

The antenna and equipment at the top of the bridge (55.8) marks a weather station, one of four such stations that you will pass between here and Chicago. These stations are part of the Roadway Weather Information System, established by the U.S. Department of Transportation, Federal Highway Administration. You can access this system online and, for each location, find current temperature, dew point, wind speed and direction and air pressure, as well as weather data associated with visibility, lightning, tornadoes or other severe weather. These stations also send out data about pavement temperature and conditions. The information collected here keeps you safe, as officials use it to prepare warnings about dangerous driving conditions. Anybody in the world, at any time, can find out about the weather and pavement conditions on the bridge that you just crossed. The late comedian George Carlin's Hippy Dippy Weatherman character, after giving the temperatures at the airport, would always comment, "…which is stupid because nobody lives at the airport!" Well, weather data is being collected and reported from here even though nobody lives under this bridge (as far as we know).

58: Honey Bend Herefords

Ahead on the right is Honey Bend Herefords. The Banovic family has owned this land since 1954, but they are also a four-generation mining family. Over the years, they simultaneously worked in two of Illinois' biggest industries, coal mining and agriculture. Ed Banovic raises "polled" Herefords, genetically modified Herefords that don't grow horns. Ed currently has thirty mother cows from which he sells embryos and calves to other breeders. Read more about this family at 59S.

Traveling through Illinois

Honey Bend farm has changed over sixty years, but the same family still keeps it growing. *Ted Cable.*

59: College Credit

Exit 60 takes you to Carlinville's Blackburn College, a liberal arts college where students work together like a community inside and outside of class. Blackburn is the "least expensive, private four-year residential institution in the state of Illinois," mainly due to the student work program that was established in 1913. The work program allows those students financially incapable of attending college to work for part of their tuition. Students work a minimum of 160 hours each semester helping with services around campus. This work then helps offset the high cost of a college education. Blackburn is one of only seven "work colleges" in the country and the only student-managed one. Blackburn prides itself on the warm sense of community that students gain while working for and with their friends and faculty.

NORTHBOUND

60: Senator Express

As you pass under Route 108 here, you will be traveling the Vince Demuzio Expressway all the way to Springfield. In April 2004, this stretch of I-55 was designated the Vince Demuzio Expressway in honor of the longest-serving member of the Illinois Senate. Demuzio served in the Senate from 1974 until 2004. His advocacy for efficient roadways improved Illinois highways. Contrary to images of big-city politicians, the senator preferred to live among his friends in his small hometown of 5,700 people. He frequently traveled this stretch of I-55 as he made the commute from Carlinville to the capitol. When Senator Demuzio died of colon cancer in 2004, his wife, Deanna, was chosen unanimously to fill his vacancy. She extended the family tradition of serving Illinois until 2010.

63: Tornado Alley

If you are traveling on a blustery day, especially between the months of April and June, you may be scanning the skies for funnel clouds. On average, forty-two tornadoes travel through Illinois each year, and many have crossed I-55. On June 1, 1999, a tornado with a two-hundred-yard-wide damage path hit the rest area just ahead (at mile 65) on your right. The F-3 tornado overturned six tractor-trailer trucks and killed one driver and injured four others before it traveled farther northeast for ten miles. The National Weather Service defines an F-3 tornado (on a scale of 0 to 5) as a strong damaging tornado with 136- to 165-mile-per-hour winds.

Some tornados can leave a path of destruction up to one mile wide and more than sixty miles long, and they can form during any month. Meteorologists advise that when drivers on highways spot a tornado, they shouldn't attempt to outdrive the unpredictable twisting mass of debris. Tornadoes can weave back and forth over a road and change directions quickly. They suggest that if it is visible and far away, you should drive at right angles to avoid it. Drivers shouldn't park under bridges or overpasses since the winds can actually be more severe as they rush under these spots. Rather, you should look for a nearby business where you could take shelter. If no businesses are nearby, park your car, move away from it so it doesn't roll over on you, lie facedown in any low-lying area like a ditch or culvert and cross your arms over your head for protection from flying debris.

Traveling through Illinois

66: You Can Count on Corn

To I-55 travelers, it is no surprise that agriculture is Illinois largest industry, contributing billions of dollars to the state each year. You could probably guess that corn is the largest contributor to these agricultural benefits. Illinois ranks second only to Iowa in the production of corn. In 2010, Illinois produced a record 13.4 billion bushels, with a record average yield of 180 bushels/acre.

What can come from a single bushel of corn? A bushel of corn fed to livestock produces about six pounds of retail beef, thirteen pounds of pork, twenty pounds of chicken or twenty-eight pounds of catfish. A bushel also can yield thirty-two pounds of cornstarch, 2.8 gallons of ethanol fuel or thirty-three pounds of corn syrup—enough to sweeten more than four hundred cans of soda. Two types of corn are grown in the fields along the highway, sweet corn and field corn. Each is used for different products. Sweet corn is harvested when it is young and the kernel is juicy. An ear of sweet corn has about eight hundred kernels in sixteen rows. If not eaten right off the cob, sweet corn is sent to processors, where it is canned or frozen. Field corn is stored and dried in one of the many grain elevators or silver farm storage bins you pass along the highway. From there, it is taken to mills, where it is made into feed; ethanol plants, where it is made into fuel (Illinois sends more corn to ethanol plants than any other state); ports, where it is shipped overseas; or other industries, where it is put to surprising uses.

More than 4,200 supermarket products contain corn or corn byproducts. If your car is packed for a trip, it probably contains a cornucopia of corn products, including toothpaste, chewing gum, aspirin, catsup and mustard (on your corn-fed beef hamburger, of course), peanut butter (in that candy bar you had to have at the gas station), soda, coffee, tea, plastics, cosmetics, crayons, shoe polish and ink. Even without a suitcase, you'll still find corn in your road map, spark plugs, tires and fuel.

70: Wind Power

On the right, the Gob Knob turbine produces energy for the Rural Electric Convenience Cooperative, based in Auburn. In 2009, the lone windmill was constructed on a "gob pile," an area where coal was discarded. The first wind farm in Illinois was completed in 2005. This is just the first of many turbines that you will see if you drive north to the Chicago area.

NORTHBOUND

71: So God Made a Farmer

In tribute to those farmers who work the land all along this route, we pause in our admiration and share an excerpt from Paul Harvey's address to the 1987 American Farm Bureau Federation Convention:

> *And on the eighth day, God looked down on his planned paradise and said I need a caretaker—So God made a Farmer. God said I need somebody willing to get up before dawn, milk the cows, work all day in the field, milk cows again, eat supper then go to town and stay past midnight at a meeting of the school board—So God made a Farmer. I need somebody with arms strong enough to wrestle a calf and yet gentle enough to deliver his own grandchild; somebody to call hogs, tame cantankerous machinery, come home hungry, have to await lunch until his wife's done feeding visiting ladies, then tell the ladies to be sure and come back real soon, and mean it—So God made a Farmer. God said I need somebody willing to sit up all night with a newborn colt, and watch it die, then dry his eyes and say, "Maybe next year." I need somebody who can shape an axe handle from a persimmon sprout, shoe a horse with a hunk of car tire, who can make a harness out of hay wire, feed sacks, and shoe straps, who at planting time and harvest season will finish his forty-hour week by Tuesday noon and then, paining from tractor back, will put in another 72 hours—So God made a Farmer...It had to be somebody who'd plow deep and straight and not cut corners; somebody to seed, weed, feed, and breed, and rake and disk and plow and plant and tie the fleece and strain the milk and replenish the self-feeder and a hard week's work with a five-mile drive to church. Somebody who would bale a family together with the soft, strong bonds of sharing; who would laugh and then sigh, and reply with smiling eyes when his son says he want to spend his life doing what dad does—So God made a Farmer.*

75: Changing Fashion

The old mansion, ahead on the right at mile 76, only slightly resembles its original appearance when it was built in the 1860s. Just as changing fashion styles define historical eras, the architectural styles of buildings and homes create their own fashion timelines. Two fires, many owners and almost 150 years of wear have made today's mansion almost unrecognizable when compared to the design that Elijah E. Myers created in 1863 for landowner Lewis Thomas. Myers constructed this home with Italianate villa features that were popular

TRAVELING THROUGH ILLINOIS

The west side of the Lewis Thomas mansion, 1874, as seen from the highway. *From the Illustrated Atlas of Montgomery County, Illinois.*

in the 1850s and '60s. This mansion was once dressed with arched windows, eaves that dripped with intricately carved brackets and an ornate top on the tower. At the top of the tower, the year 1888 is carved in stone. This is the year a fire destroyed much of the home; when it was rebuilt, Italianate had been booted from the architectural runway and replaced by Queen Anne, the new fashionista of the time. Just like fluffy perms and parachute pants replaced straight hair and bellbottoms, Queen Anne's square windows straightened some Italian curves and freed the eaves of brackets.

Read more at 76S about the history of this impressive estate that once covered 970 acres here in Montgomery County.

77: In the Distance

Silver grain bins glisten across the expansive fields. If you look just to the right of the bins at mile 78 ahead, you can see the stacks of Springfield's City, Water, Light and Power (CWLP) plant sending up clouds of smoke sixteen miles away. They look tiny from here, but the smokestacks are the three tallest structures in the Springfield area, rising 500, 450 and 440 feet in the air, respectively. You'll learn more about this plant when you see it up close ahead at mile 93.

It's amazing how far in the distance you can see, in either direction, on your drive along I-55. Some people interpret central Illinois as an empty, lonely landscape that spreads out widely and fails to hold them close. Others feel a beauty where cropland meets the horizon. Keith Jacobshagen wrote in

Northbound

The Changing Prairie "If one is to understand the beauty of this place, the old answers just won't do."

If old answers won't do, what are the new answers? Are they the long, spectacular sunrises and sunsets, the islands of clouds in the blue sea overhead, the way the wind bends the grain and grasses into waves or the way you can set the cruise control and relax a bit on the "literally" open highway, leaving tense shoulders for those who maneuver endless turns through narrow forest interstates and must fear worn brake pads on steep mountain highways. Here, those who understand this lovely emptiness will find peace and beauty that they will find incomparable to anywhere else.

79: Divernon

The town of Divernon was named in 1887 by resident H.C. Barnes, for the character Diana Vernon, the heroine of Sir Walter Scott's 1817 novel, *Rob Roy*. "Di" Vernon was the love interest of the main character, Frank Osbaldistone (surprisingly, Rob Roy is not the main character in the novel *Rob Roy*). According to an 1870 *Macmillan's Magazine* literature review, Diana Vernon was the "synonym for ever of a beautiful and masculine-tempered girl, who loves field sports, sets etiquette at defiance, and consults only her own inclinations." She was a bold and self-reliant woman of "very powerful mind" and "unusual literary accomplishments."

Highways such as I-55 are settings in many life stories. They are runways to fly independently from a birthplace and sturdy threads that repeatedly lead back home. They are settings of comings and goings in our lives—of saying hello and saying goodbye. Here follows a scene from *Rob Roy* where Di Vernon and Frank must part along the road.

> *"Yes, Frank," she said "for ever! There is a gulf between us—a gulf of absolute perdition;—where we go you must not follow;—what we do, you must not share in. Farewell!—Be happy!"*
>
> *In the attitude in which she bent, from her horse, a Highland pony, her face, not perhaps altogether unwillingly, touched mine. She pressed my hand, while the tear that trembled in her eye found its way to my cheek instead of her own. It was a moment never to be forgotten—inexpressibly bitter yet mixed with a sensation of pleasure so deeply soothing and affecting, as at once to unlock all the flood-gates of the heart...and putting their horses to a brisk pace, they were soon far distant from the place where I stood."*

83: Sweet Settlement

A few miles back, you entered Sangamon County. Less than a mile to the left of you, Sugar Creek follows the same course of your journey as it makes its way to Lake Springfield. It was along this creek's banks, and near this area, that Robert Pulliam built the first pioneer settlement in Sangamon County in 1817. Pulliam was a Virginia native who founded a stream of settlements as he slowly made his way west until he arrived in the Sangamon Valley, a fruitful, mixed landscape of streams, timber and prairie. Pulliam built his cabin beside Sugar Creek among a grove of sugar maples that he tapped for his sweetener. In the nearby fields, his cattle grazed on the thick prairie grasses. You can read more about the origin of the name "Sangamon" at mile 97.

86: Land of Lincoln

In a few miles, you will enter Springfield, the capital of Illinois and home to many stories of its most famous resident, Abraham Lincoln. This is the city where Lincoln shared a law office, moved into his first home with Mary Todd, raised his boys, served as a legislator, learned he had been elected the sixteenth president, delivered an intensely emotional farewell address to his friends as he left for the White House and returned four years later on a funeral train to be buried in his beloved city. (Read more about the funeral train at mile 106S.) Visitors can tour Lincoln's home, the Lincoln Presidential Library and Museum, the Lincoln-Herndon Law Office, the Old State Capitol, the New State Capitol and Lincoln's tomb and even see the pew where he and his family sat for church each Sunday.

Reminders that he lived here abound. Patrons check out books from the Lincoln Public Library, students attend Lincoln Land Community College and golfers play at Lincoln Greens Golf Course. Everyone can play at Lincoln Park. Road passengers hail taxis from the Lincoln Cab Company, while rail passengers take the "Ann Rutledge" (named after a friend from his youth). The list of Lincoln-inspired names extends to more than forty businesses with the name Lincoln listed in the Springfield phone book. Lincoln was quoted as saying, "I like to see a man proud of the place in which he lives and to so live that the place he lives is proud of him." Clearly, his town is proud of him.

Native Springfield poet Vachel Lindsay, known as the "prairie troubadour," sang mournfully of Lincoln's ghost that still inhabits Springfield. In

"Abraham Lincoln Walks at Midnight (in Springfield, Illinois)," he portrays a figure who cannot sleep for all of the unrest in the world:

> *It is portentous, and a thing of state*
> *That here at midnight, in our little town*
> *A mourning figure walks, and will not rest,*
> *Near the old court-house pacing up and down.*
>
> *Or by his homestead, or in shadowed yards*
> *He lingers where his children used to play,*
> *Or through the market, on the well-worn stones*
> *He stalks until the dawn-stars burn away.*
>
> *A bronzed, lank man! His suit of ancient black,*
> *A famous high top-hat and plain worn shawl*
> *Make him the quaint great figure that men love,*
> *The prairie-lawyer, master of us all.*

While the state's slogan, "Land of Lincoln," is displayed on its license plates, Springfield is the land where Lincoln left most of his footprints. If you don't have time to veer off the highway into the heart of Lincoln history, you can read more about his life at the rest area near mile 104.

89: Lake Springfield

Cruising across this bridge, you may catch a glimpse of boats cruising Lake Springfield. But this lake is more than a place to enjoy some sun and cool breezes. This lake was built to provide Springfield with an ample water supply and to create the steam that rises from the smokestacks you'll see ahead. In 1930, as Springfield's population began to outgrow the water supply it absorbed from the Sangamon River (mile 102), citizens voted to dig a man-made lake in the Sugar Creek Valley. Some residents, however, weren't so happy about creating the new water source. Leander Shoup used his shotgun to hold off sheriff's deputies for several days before surrendering his land to progress. On July 12, 1935, the lake was dedicated with a grand ceremony. Waters from the Atlantic and Pacific Oceans and twenty-six other sources, including the Fountain of Youth (St. Augustine, Florida), were poured into the fresh new lake.

TRAVELING THROUGH ILLINOIS

90: Sky Wars

Hilton Hotel: Springfield's pinnacle on the prairie. *LuAnn Cadden.*

Directly ahead, you can see the tallest building in Springfield, according to an employee of the Springfield Hilton. The thirty-story-tall downtown hotel rises like a lighthouse from the prairie ocean. Only the state capitol building, which you can see to its left, competes with the Hilton's towering presence in the empty prairie skyline—literally competes. After the Hilton was completed in 1973, it was found to be taller than the state capitol building. Shortly after its construction, a flagpole was erected on the capitol building that enabled the capitol to reclaim its star status as the tallest building in Springfield at 405 feet. In order to secure this "lofty" status, legislators passed a city statute that noted that no building in Springfield can ever be built taller than the capitol. But in a final counterattack to reclaim the skies, an emergency antenna was placed on the Hilton's roof—a final blow in the sky wars saga. Read more about the state capitol at 101S.

93: Prairie Power

Ahead, you'll get a close-up view of the smokestacks of the City, Water, Light and Power (CWLP) plant that you saw way back at mile 78. Most power here is generated by coal, and all the coal used here comes from Illinois mines like the Viper Mine (mile 111), just north of here. Just before the power plant, on your right, you can see a tiny inlet of Lake Springfield, once again. The shorter black stack that isn't smoking was the plant's original smokestack from 1936. Read more about this power plant at 98S.

Northbound

95: Look-alike Lake

Just ahead on your left is the Illinois Department of Transportation headquarters. You might spot anglers fishing and geese feeding along the slender lake between the building and I-55. Lake Lorenz was named after Francis S. Lorenz, the State Department of Public Works director when the building was constructed in the early 1960s. Many Springfield residents will proudly tell you that the lake is shaped like the state of Illinois. But this clever shape may have been inspired by the original lay of the land or may have just been coincidence. The lake was excavated as a borrow pit during building construction. Aerial photos show that the land between the highway and the proposed DOT building was naturally shaped like Illinois

Illinois-shaped field before construction, June 15, 1965. *Illinois Department of Transportation, Aerial Services Section.*

Traveling through Illinois

Illinois Department of Transportation and Lake Lorenz, June 12, 2007. *Illinois Department of Transportation, Aerial Services Section.*

before the lake was built. The island in the middle of the lake was built in 2006 as a place where geese and ducks could find refuge from predators roaming the shoreline. Perhaps we could start a rumor that this central island represents the centrally located capital city of Springfield.

97: Say Sang-a-mon

Since mile 77, you've been traveling through Sangamon County. Sangamon is oftentimes mispronounced by visitors. That seems fitting since the name itself likely came from misconstruing a pronunciation. In 1721, a Jesuit priest named Charlevoix recorded the first variation of this name when

Northbound

he passed by the Sangamon River. He recorded it as the Saguimont River. It is believed that his Ojibway Indian guide may have said, "Sagi-ong," meaning "river-mouth," as they passed by, and Charlevoix, like many early explorers, recorded what he thought he heard. However you say it, this name, Sangamon, is seen throughout the area. Springfield once boasted the *Sangamo Journal*, Sangamo Electric Company and Sangamon State University. Ahead you'll have the opportunity to exit on Sangamon Avenue (mile 100) and to cross the Sangamon River (mile 103).

100: The Route to Sangamo Town

Here you pass Sangamon Avenue, the last exit to Springfield. Back in 1825, another route northwest of Springfield took travelers to Sangamo Town, a town that was active with river commerce between 1824 and 1845. Today, all that is left of this town are woods and fields. No traces remain of Charles Broadwell's or William Porter's mills, the few stores and the homes of the fifty residents (including a grandson of Alexander Hamilton). When you cross the Sangamon River in a few miles, imagine the town seven miles directly to the west. Founded just three years after Springfield, Sangamo Town competed with Springfield to gain the county seat in the 1820s. Five commissioners came out to tour both towns. After being wined and dined in Springfield, the commissioners asked a guide to take them to Sangamo Town. Their guide took them all right. He took them through the most difficult route possible, even winding back in loops through the brushiest, muddiest, most exasperating journey the commissioners could endure. When the frustrated and weary politicians returned to Springfield, they unanimously declared Springfield the county seat, and Sangamo Town lost a battle from which it would never recover.

102: Sangamon River

Just ahead, you will cross the historic Sangamon River. Abraham Lincoln's family settled along the Sangamon when he was twenty-one years old. From 1831 to 1837, Lincoln lived along this river at New Salem and navigated it by flatboat. Can you imagine a steamship navigating down this narrow river? This shallow, winding, sandbar-dotted, snag-infested little river carried the fifteen-ton steamboat *Talisman* from St. Louis to Springfield in 1832. After navigating the Mississippi and then the Illinois, the *Talisman* floated into the Sangamon. This accomplishment raised hopes that the Sangamon would become a highway of commerce for central Illinois. In grand celebration, residents lined the banks of the Sangamon cheering and greeting the steamship, local poets penned congratulatory verses and a women's group organized a celebration ball. The local *Sangamo Journal* proudly reported that "Springfield can no longer be considered an inland town." But pride soon turned to embarrassment and disappointment when the river level dropped dramatically and forced the steamship to back down the muddy waterway. Needless to say, Springfield's hopes of becoming a commercial river town went "down with the ship."

Abe Lincoln thought that if the Sangamon couldn't adapt to steamship travel, he would invent a device to help the ships adapt to the river. His Patent No. 6469 (the only patent by a U.S. president) demonstrated how boats could be lifted over shoals. But his device was never manufactured, and the history-rich Sangamon River never became commerce-rich. No other steamers attempted this trip, and Springfield remained an "inland town."

104: Sherman

It seems that this little town situated just five miles north of Springfield would naturally have been named for William Tecumseh Sherman, Lincoln's friend and the famous Union army general in the Civil War. The fact that the Illinois State Military Museum is at this exit might reinforce that belief. But this town's name was literally just pulled out of a hat. In 1858, four men platted Sherman. Town founders Cornelius Flagg, Joseph Ledlie, Virgil Hickox and David Sherman all dropped their names into a hat, and Sherman emerged the namesake. Sherman's population boomed in the early twentieth century when Italians settled here to work in local coal mines. By 1959, one hundred years after David Sherman's name was drawn, the village had grown to 209 people and was officially incorporated. Today, about 3,500 residents have settled in Sherman, and each year, thousands of others come here to see the Labor Day Rail Charity Golf Classic, the second-longest-running golf tournament in LPGA history.

NORTHBOUND

106: Rolling Along the Railroad

To your right run the rails of the interstate's transportation predecessor and current partner in moving people and products. Between 1852 and 1853, this track was laid between Springfield to Bloomington. By 1860, the Alton & Sangamon Railroad had become the Chicago & Alton Railroad and extended from East St. Louis to Chicago. In July 1851, Springfield's *Daily Journal* described the anticipated line that was growing northward from Alton:

> *The ties and iron for over one half of the road are upon the ground; and the balance of the ties and iron are being received—(the ties from Cumberland River, and the iron from New Orleans, where they are in readiness for shipment.) The ties are all of red cedar, except every seventh or "spike tie," is of white or post oak, and of double size...The iron is the H rail, weighing a fraction over fifty-six pounds per yard. The ties are laid thirty inches from centre to centre.*

Laborers, mostly Irish immigrants, laid nearly two miles of track each week. Read more about these Irish rail workers at 148S. Today, you probably will see at least one freight train carrying crops or an Amtrak train carrying folks between the Mississippi River and Lake Michigan.

109: Tree Farm

Just ahead, near mile 110, you'll see neat rows of young trees growing on Harold Carter's property. Although a builder by trade, Carter grows and sells these saplings as a hobby, sharing his time and talent to help beautify this community of which he's proud. He has transported many trees to the historic bed-and-breakfast atop Elkhart Hill (mile 116) and other locations within a forty-mile radius. In 1977, Carter and his wife had a complete landscaping business here along nostalgic Route 66. Today, he sells trees (mostly oaks and maples) from his home and delivers them to city parks, municipal buildings, businesses and private homes. Seventeenth-century theologian Thomas Fuller wrote, "He that plants trees loves others besides himself." Carter embodies that statement, saying that he truly enjoys planting trees for his friends and neighbors. His property includes a borrow pit for I-55, like the ones described back at mile 54. His interstate pond is a nicely landscaped home for frogs, dragonflies, ducks and the swans he placed there for the drivers of old Route 66 to enjoy. "Acts of creation are ordinarily reserved for gods and poets," said conservationist Aldo Leopold, adding, "To plant a pine, one need only own a shovel." Carter carries out his acts of creation armed with a backhoe, more than thirty-five years of experience and plenty of love for his hometown of Williamsville.

110: Viper Mine

The two structures seen on the horizon to the right mark the Viper Mine. The angled structure is a conveyer that brings coal to the top of the cylinder-shaped silo where the coal is stored until it is removed from the bottom, and then it is washed in a preparation plant to remove rocks and other impurities. Coal is then conveyed to the top of the second silo and stored until it is shipped to the customers. The buildings here immediately next to I-55 mark the mine opening, which provides direct access to a recent extension of the mine. This puts workers closer to the remaining 33 million tons of coal below you right now. Notice the silver conveyor belt structure

Springfield coal miners, 1892. *Sangamon Valley Collection, Lincoln Library.*

that parallels the highway for the next two miles. It can carry eight hundred tons of raw coal per hour, twenty-four hours a day, from this mine entrance to the silos, where it is stored and washed.

Viper Mine is a room-and-pillar operation. In such mines, coal is removed from areas called rooms. Pillars of unmined coal are left between the rooms to support the roof. Depending on the size of rooms and pillars, the amount of coal removed from the production areas will range from 40 to 70 percent. Enough pillars must be left to prevent the farmland above from subsiding. When going under railroads and highways, even more coal pillars are left in place to support the roof. Viper Mine produces twelve thousand tons of coal per day. The coal is transported to customers in Illinois, with electric utilities accounting for 58 percent of coal sales. The largest customer is Springfield's City, Water, Light and Power (CWLP). The Viper Mine has grown since its opening in 1982 and has now extended under I-55. It might startle you to know that dozens of miners, headlamps beaming, are working in the darkness three hundred feet beneath you right now.

112: Settling Logan

You have just entered Logan County. As a representative of the Committee on Counties, Abraham Lincoln introduced the bill to establish this county and named it after his fellow legislator and friend Dr. John Logan in 1839. In 1818, the same year that Illinois became a state, settlers from Kentucky found the banks of the Sangamon River a perfect place to build their cabins. However, seasonal flooding soon drove the settlers out of the floodplain and up to Elkhart Hill, a pinnacle on the prairie. Just ahead, you'll see Elkhart Hill.

113: Here's a Hill

For many miles, you have driven through land that is as flat as a tabletop. But here is a hill! The wooded hill rising above the town of Elkhart is 777 feet above sea level and is the tallest hill between Chicago and St. Louis. The only other "hills" you will encounter between Chicago and St. Louis are man-made features such as the spoils of a strip mine or mammoth landfill mountains. Glaciers scraped and flattened the land as they moved south. They created Elkhart Hill by leaving behind this pile of rock and soil as they melted and retreated.

Traveling through Illinois

You are one of a multitude of travelers, including many historic figures, who have passed by this hill. An ancient path crosses the hill. Native Americans used this path for seasonal migrations and for hunting and trading. Fur traders and pioneers used it, as did herds of migrating buffalo. It became known as Edwards Trace (22N) after Ninian Edwards led nearly four hundred men along this trail up to Fort Clark near present-day Peoria during the War of 1812. Later, it would become a stagecoach route. Circuit-riding lawyers Abraham Lincoln and Stephen Douglas used the trail and would often stop here. Eventually, a railroad station replaced the stagecoach stop. Route 66 brought even more folks past Elkhart Hill.

A seventh-generation family farm sits on top of the hill today. Lincoln visited this farm, as did the Drakes (of Chicago's Drake Hotel fame), and presidential candidate Adlai Stevenson wrote a campaign speech on the porch, saying that the peaceful setting cleared his thoughts and the view inspired his words. The farm is open for weddings, special events, tours and as a bed-and-breakfast.

115: Elkhart Grain Company

On your right is the Elkhart Grain Company. Here the spoils of the prairie fields are gathered from farmers who live within about a ten-mile radius. Grain elevators are the link between the fields and the companies, which turn crops into multiple products. At mile 138, you'll pass the town of Atlanta and the J.W. Hawes Grain Elevator Museum. This 1904 grain elevator, listed on the National Register of Historic Places, has been renovated to display and interpret the cycle of grain from field to market. Read more about the Elkhart Grain Company at 118S.

118: Broadwell

William Broadwell and Jacob Eisiminger platted the village of Broadwell in 1856 as a railroad town linking Chicago and Springfield. Jacob Eisiminger declined having the village named after him, stating that the new village would be handicapped with such an unusual name. While Broadwell moved on to Kansas, the Eisiminger family became longtime merchants, postmasters and schoolteachers here, with the last Eisiminger dying in 2006.

Northbound

The Pig Hip Restaurant was a favorite stop for many Route 66 travelers. Today, only a sign remains to remember the Pig Hip. Read more about this iconic restaurant at 120S.

121: Slowing Water

Just before mile 122, on the right, you can see wide strips of grass weaving through the crop fields. Farmers create these grass waterways to slow the rainwater that runs off the fields. Rainwater erodes away the land and moves soil particles into streams and rivers. Soil erosion by wind and water is inevitable, but farmers reduce these forces by applying techniques to slow the water runoff and hold soil particles in place. Cropland covered in grass erodes at a rate four thousand times less than a bare field. Strategies such as planting these grass strips in drainages, contour plowing (making furrows across the slope), leaving crop residue on the surface, creating raised ridges called "terraces" that catch rainwater and allow it to soak into the soil or leaving a buffer of vegetation along streams are ways farmers reduce erosion and save our precious soil.

123: The First Lincoln

Many counties, towns, parks and schools are named for Abraham Lincoln, but Lincoln, Illinois, is the only one named for him before he became president. The founders named this city after the Springfield lawyer who helped them incorporate their new town. At 135S, read more about Lincoln University and how Abe "fruitfully" christened this town himself.

126: Kerner's Curve

Just before mile 127, I-55 veers to the right, and I-155 travels due north to Peoria. If former Governor Otto Kerner had had his way, I-55 would travel north to Peoria rather than to Bloomington. In 1965, citizens feuded over whether the interstate should be routed northeast along US 66 or north through Peoria to I-80. Citizens were outraged when Kerner announced that he wanted to switch the interstate route overlaying Route 66 to a new road to Peoria, Illinois. This proposed roundabout way of getting to Chicago

Traveling through Illinois

became known as "Kerner's Curve." If Kerner's Curve had become a reality and I-55 had been built outside the Route 66 corridor, would Route 66 roadside restaurants, gas stations and quirky tourist spots have faded faster or more slowly? Would Bloomington-Normal have prospered? Today, we have the best of both plans as I-155 takes Kerner's route.

127: Saving Seeds

Here along the highway, prairie wildflowers bloom. You may have noticed the round white blossoms of Queen Anne's lace lining the roadside, but in this area, purple coneflowers, wild bergamot, brown-eyed Susans, milkweed and others display their colorful petals.

Wild bergamot, resembling a small, purple firework explosion atop a tall, leafy stem, makes a healthy tea. Purple coneflower, resembling a badminton birdie, with the round top and dark-pink petals radiating downward, is well known as Echinacea by healthy folks, who take it to boost their immune

Louise Behrend and her students from Six Mile School pose with the milkweed pods they collected during World War II. *McLean County Historical Society.*

system. For centuries, it has been used as a remedy for more ailments than any other plant. Indians and pioneers used it to heal snakebites, stings, headaches, toothaches, sores, ulcers, swelling, inflammation and many more ailments. Today, it is nicely packed into pills on most pharmaceutical shelves and is still used by millions of Americans, especially during cold and flu season.

The milkweed plant also saved lives, but in a completely different way. During World War II, schoolchildren collected milkweed pods, and the buoyant floss on its seed was used to stuff life jackets for soldiers. The government sent a call out to America's children and asked them to scour roadsides, railroad tracks and pastures to find the precious seed that was once looked on as a common weed. Just north of here, in McLean County, schoolchildren collected 1,900 sacks of milkweed pods in the fall of 1944. The bags were taken north to Towanda, stored in two steel corn bins and then shipped by rail to a milkweed floss processing plant in Petoskey, Michigan. Six Mile School, in the northeast corner of Normal Township, found most of its milkweed around Lake Bloomington and the Chicago & Alton Railroad tracks and collected the most seed in the county (110 sacks).

Milkweed isn't just a lifesaver for humans; it also is necessary for the survival of the monarch butterfly, the Illinois state insect. Here among these prairie plants, you may glimpse its orange and black wings as it feeds on the nectar of these wildflowers or lays its eggs on the milkweed plant.

133: Winds of Change

On the far, far left, you can get a glimpse of what is to come. Wind turbines create a wind farm that captures breezes and converts them into electricity for communities near and far. This newer technology has changed the landscape of I-55 incredibly in the past five years. You will see many more wind farms as you travel north and will get much closer views of the turbines that, at some points, nearly line the highway. You can read more about wind farms at mile 206.

135: Lawndale

To the left is a historic elevator with a "Faultless Feed" sign from the Route 66 era. The Faultless Milling Company began producing animal feed in

Springfield in 1881, and now its feedbags are collectors' items. In 1977, seven witnesses reported that two giant birds passed over Lawndale; one of them grabbed ten-year-old Marlon Lowe from his backyard where he was playing with two other boys. The bird grasped the boy's shoulder with its talons and carried him two feet off the ground as Marlon's mother screamed frantically. The bird dropped the struggling Marlon nearby. This case gained national media attention and put Lawndale on the map, at least among cryptozoologists—researchers who study animals considered to be mythical by mainstream biologists.

136: Cottonwood Commerce

If you are driving along this stretch of highway in winter, snow may be flying past your windshield, but if you are passing through in June, you may also see flurries. A small cluster of eastern cottonwood trees, on your right, sends tiny brown seeds parachuting by cottony hairs across the highway like a summer snowstorm. Notice how the heart-shaped cottonwood leaves seem to be continually moving. Cottonwood leaves constantly flutter because they have flat, rather than round, stems that make them twirl and twist wildly in the slightest breeze.

Indian tribes shaped these tree trunks into sturdy canoes for their trips of commerce and companionship across the state. With hot coals, they would first burn the trunk and then scrape out the charred wood to sculpt their dugout canoes. Plains and Prairie Indian tribes found cottonwood canoes sturdier than the birch-bark canoes of the northern woodlands. Cottonwoods still contribute to commerce. If you stopped for an ice cream treat during your drive today, you may have held a cottonwood stick in your hand. The wood is used for such things as ice cream sticks, kites, veneer, baskets, pulpwood and fuel. These lively trees are fast growers but short-lived. Years from now, this stand may be gone, but most likely, somewhere along I-55 you'll still see these seed aviators planting wood products across the prairie.

You will also notice the tall *Phragmites* grass along the highway for these few miles. Read more about this invasive plant at 261S.

NORTHBOUND

138: Have a Nice Day!

A yellow water tower with a smiley face rises above the village of Atlanta, so-called because the founder liked Atlanta, Georgia. The town was originally named Xenia by settlers from Xenia, Ohio. Just behind the water tower is the red top of the J.W. Hawes Grain Elevator Museum, mentioned back at mile 115. Atlanta rose to prominence as a railroad town and then as a Route 66 town. Read more at 139S about Atlanta's bustling boomtown days in the 1850s.

If you are looking for a quirky Route 66–era photo opportunity, exit here and have your photo taken with Tall Paul, a nineteen-foot statue of a man holding a huge hot dog. You can also take an interesting self-guided interpretive tour at the Hawes Grain Elevator Museum, or you can call ahead for a guided tour in the summer months

141: The Most Productive County

McLean County was established on Christmas Day in 1830. It is named for John McLean, the first representative in Congress from Illinois (1818–19) and United States senator (1824–25 and 1829–30). It is the largest county in Illinois, with a land area of 1,184 square miles, making it larger than Rhode Island. McLean County's deep black prairie soil is some of the richest and most productive soil in the world. Because of that rich soil, McLean County produces both more corn and more soybeans than any other county in the United States. McLean Stevenson, star of *M*A*S*H* and other popular TV shows, was born and raised among the fields of corn and beans in McLean County.

142: Going Up!

If you look carefully at the road at this mile, you may notice that you are ever so slightly driving up an incline. You are climbing up a moraine—a long, sloping ridge that formed from fourteen to twenty-five thousand years ago when large ice sheets shoved glacial till into a ridge as they moved south. Glacial sheets moved like snow shovels, scraping and pushing debris ahead of them to deposit in a ridge of soil.

The hill in Elkhart, at mile 113, was a noticeable ridge of till left from the glacier, but the moraine you are climbing is many miles long. It is difficult

Traveling through Illinois

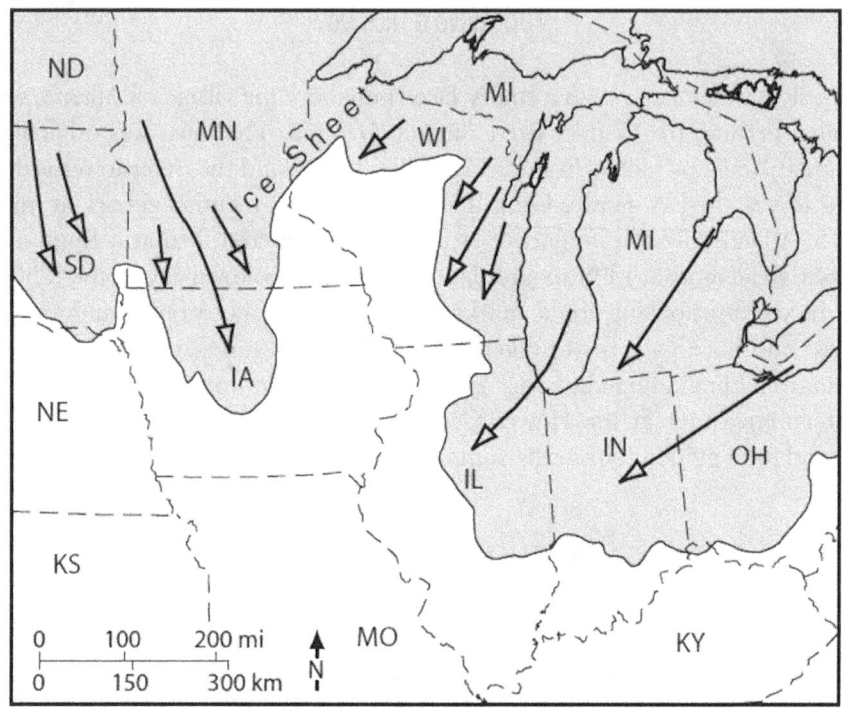

Glacial ice sheets scraped the land and deposited ridges of till across the flat prairie. *University of Illinois Board of Trustees, Illinois State Geological Survey,* ©2013.

to notice that you are on a moraine, but satellite photos of Illinois reveal long, curved ridges of glacial till that stretch across the northern half of the state. Just like drivers who start in Kansas City and drive a flat, straight line all the way to Denver without noticing the almost five-thousand-foot climb in elevation, you are also rising up, toward the peak of the Bloomington Moraine, which will crest on I-55 on the north side of Bloomington.

144: Dixie Truckers Home

The Dixie Truckers Home at exit 145 was once a family-owned business that operated as "home" for travelers for seventy-five years. It began in 1928 as a mechanic's garage from which J.P. Walters and John Geske sold sandwiches to truckers and motorists traveling on Route 66 at a counter with six stools. During the Great Depression, beggars and hoboes who jumped off the train

Northbound

would come to the back door and were never turned away hungry. Within a few years, the site had built a full restaurant, cabins for overnight stays and a cattle pen where cattle could exercise while the truckers ate. Until World War II, it even offered live entertainment and music on weekends. The owners fostered the feeling of home as they fed caravans of troops, rescued stranded motorists during winter storms and helped less fortunate travelers. Although now under new ownership, after four generations of being run by the same family, the new Dixie Truckers Home still serves travelers on old Route 66 as well as folks traveling on I-55.

147: Sirup for Sale

Another family business booms down the road from the Dixie Truckers Home. Just ahead, you'll see a sign on the left that advertises "Pure Maple Sirup" for sale. This is no typographical error. The family chooses to use the original spelling of sirup found in the Webster's Dictionary, and over the years, I-55 and Route 66 customers readily associate this spelling with

Tapping for maple sirup at Funks Grove. *LuAnn Cadden.*

the famous pure maple Funk family sirup. The Funk family has been selling sirup from their maple grove since 1824, soon after their patriarch, Isaac, discovered the thick grove of maple trees. Isaac possibly started the longest-running family business along Route 66. Over the next few miles, you'll see the thick grove of trees along the left side of the highway. Although this grove seems oddly planted among fields of corn and soybeans, it represents the original Illinois landscape—a patchwork of lush prairies and rich stands of timber. Lafayette Funk was cofounder and director of the Chicago Union Stockyards and served as an Illinois senator. You can read more about the Funk family and early Route 66 ahead at the rest area near mile 149.

149: Halfway There

If you've been traveling from St. Louis heading for Chicago, you're halfway there! This rest area is situated two and a half hours between both cities. The information at this area is worth a stop to learn about this historic transportation crossroad. Indoor and outdoor exhibits tell stories of the early auto era, Route 66, the history of Bloomington and Normal and Isaac Funk's settling of this area. This is also the longest entrance to a rest stop along Illinois I-55. Okay, so that claim to fame doesn't sound too impressive, but this road to restrooms is visually pleasant. Since only one building serves both the northbound and southbound routes, you'll have to travel under the interstate and meander through a scenic grove of trees before you finally get there.

151: Home Tweet Home

Look for a box on the back of the rest area sign on your left, the southbound side of I-55. This is a nesting box for American kestrels, a small colorful falcon. A group called Corridors for Tomorrow placed nesting boxes like these along Illinois highways and planted wildflowers and prairie grasses in order to improve native habitat and bring Illinois' prairie interpretation a bit closer to travelers.

This blue and orange bird, sometimes called a sparrow hawk, normally nests in old woodpecker holes, but it also nests in openings in the eaves or roofs of old buildings, including the state capitol. Kestrels use nest boxes like this one when trees with cavities are in short supply. Kestrels mostly eat mice and other small mammals found in the grassy rights-of-way and medians along the highway, but they also take some sparrows and grasshoppers. You might see kestrels hovering in place like a toy helicopter above the highway, flapping their narrow pointed wings with rapid, shallow beats. You also can see them resting on signs or wires, undisturbed by the traffic rushing past.

152: Soy Tycoon

You may have noticed the "ILSOY.ORG" signs along the fence line on the right that say things like, "From Illinois soy bean fields, to Illinois roads." These signs promote freedom from dependence on foreign oil by growing soybeans to make fuel for cars, trucks and tractors. If Henry Ford were alive today, you might be driving past these rows of soybeans in a Ford Soy Car rather than merely a soy-fueled car. Ford was a huge supporter of using soy in car production. He hoped to mass-produce plastic-bodied cars made from soy, painted with soy paint and composed of soy in as many ways as possible.

Henry Ford standing by his soy car and (probably) wearing his soy suit. *From the collections of The Henry Ford.*

During the depression, he thought that a way to boost the income of those very farmers who purchased his tractors was by purchasing products from their fields and converting them into products for the road. Ford believed that "industry and agriculture are natural partners."

In the early 1930s the Ford Motor Company spent nearly $1.25 million on soybean research. Within five years, the company had incorporated soy into almost every car they manufactured. Ford's soy plastic came from the combination of soybean flour, wood flour and phenol formaldehyde plastics. But he wasn't only interested in soy for his cars. He hired chemists who produced an artificial silk from soy protein fibers, and he proudly wore his "soybean wool," a suit entirely made from soybeans. Ford also promoted soy foods. In 1934, at the World's Fair in Chicago, Ford arranged a banquet of soy for the press and even created a soy cookbook with fifty-eight recipes.

In 1941, Ford finally introduced his plastic-bodied, rust-free, dent-proof soy car. Fourteen plastic panels, each three-eighths of an inch thick, welded to a tubular steel frame that weighed between seven hundred and one thousand pounds (three-fourths the weight of a steel car). Skeptics suggested that if your car broke down, you could eat it. The jokes were reignited two years later when a goat did eat an Illinois license plate made of soybean-derived fiberboard.

But 1941 also brought World War II, which halted production of Ford's new car. He hoped to resume production after the war, but Ford passed away in 1946, and his company didn't pursue the car. Today, Ford would be happy to know that his company created the first soy-based foam used to pad car seats. It debuted in the 2008 Mustang. By 2010, more than 2 million vehicles in Ford's fleet had seats padded with the soy foam, and eventually, every one of its cars will be manufactured with the environmentally friendly filler.

155: Lone Tree

Directly to your right at this mile marker, one tree stands alone in the large field. Have you ever wondered why these single trees were left to survive or how they came to be there? Some say that the leafy canopy was a shady refuge where the farmer could rest his horses or mules in the noontime sun after a hard morning of plowing—a place to replenish himself and his animals with water and a meal. Or they could have been left to shade the cattle whose temperatures would rise dramatically as their black hides absorbed the heat of the afternoon sun. Others say that the tree was a landmark to help orient the fatigued farmer as he walked behind his plow across the flat land—it rose like a compass needle from the field and kept him focused on his course. Some of the mightiest sprawling trees with grandiose trunks may have just been too troublesome to remove. Or that lone tree may have been the lucky one, the last survivor of an old fence row after others had been taken by disease, insects or a fatal bolt of lightning.

May Theilgaard Watts, author of *Reading the Landscape of America*, believed that gophers may have been the mysterious key to how trees broke through the tough prairie sod. If early farmers, challenged by the deep and tough prairie sod, used gopher holes to plant their corn in, why couldn't opportunistic acorns use them too? She reasoned that "such a break in the sod would have made it possible for the new root thrusting downward out of the acorn to reach soil in the first season; whereas other acorns could not put out, in a single season, enough growth to penetrate soil."

158: Cargill

One mile ahead on your right, you'll see the Cargill company logo painted prominently on a white building. Here at Cargill, millions of harvested soybeans, hidden from view by white walls, await their next step in the process of getting from the fields to your pantry. Locals know this facility as the old Ralston-Purina plant. In 1948, the Cargill name was painted directly over Purina's famous checkered logo. In a twist of give and take, today Ralston-Purina is the biggest customer of Cargill. To read more about Cargill, see 160S.

159: Innovative Renovation

Just behind and to the left of the Cargill tower is a tall, skinny, gray grain elevator. What do you do with old grain storage silos after they've seen their final days of agricultural use? If you're Chris and Pam Schmick, you drill thousands of holes inside of them, add some faux rocks and turn the place into the top rock climbing gym in the world (according to the Travel Channel and Discovery Channel). This grain storage facility no longer holds grain but rather is a place where climbers scale the insides of the 65-feet concrete walls or take the old elevator up to the top and rappel 120 feet back down the

Traveling through Illinois

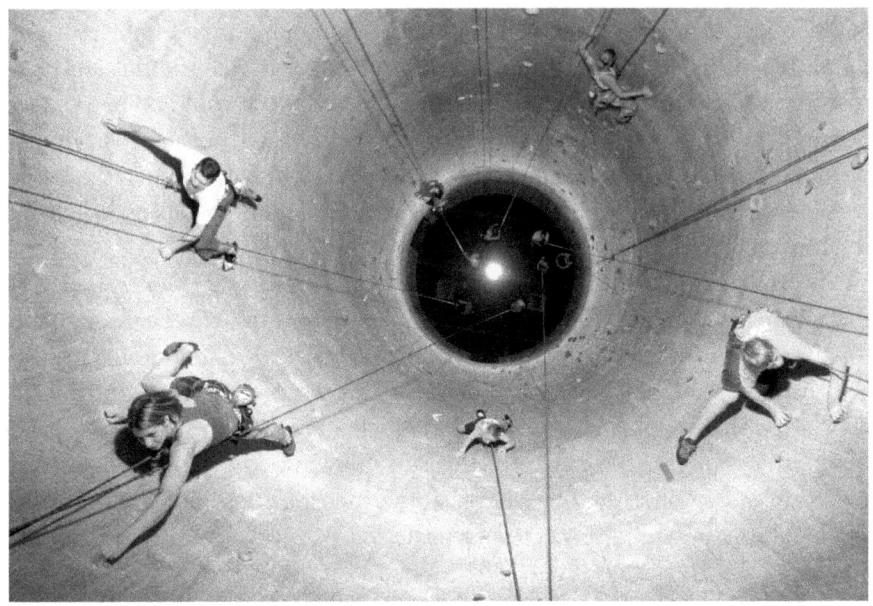

Scaling the old silo at Upper Limits. *Chris Lee.*

outside. Tons of rotten soybeans and scrap steel were hauled out, and holds, ropes and harnesses were brought in. Six months from the time they began cleaning, the Upper Limits gym opened in September 1995, offering more than 20,000 square feet of climbing. The Schmicks opened a second gym in St. Louis in 2001. One of the most exciting climbs here may have been in December 1995, when someone scaled the frozen waterfall that Chris had created down the side of the silo.

161: Higher Education

Far on the right horizon is Illinois State University's tallest residence hall. When Watterson Towers opened in 1968, it was the tallest residence hall in North America. Up to 2,200 students can reside in this sky-high home away from home. ISU was Illinois' first state university when it opened its doors in 1857 to 43 students. It began as a "normal" school, a teacher's training institution, but it has branched into a university that offers its 21,000 students studies for several career paths. The university traded its nickname "Teachers" for the "Redbirds" in 1923. The water

Northbound

tower next to the highway, on your right, sports the red-crested head of ISU's mascot, Reggie Redbird. In the 1990s, menacing human teeth appeared in Reggie's mouth to scare off those Southern Illinois Salukis and Creighton University Blue Jays. In 1989, Reggie had a new perch to "pump up" ISU sports fans when the 10,200 seat Redbird Arena opened. You can see the white crown of Redbird Arena in the distance ahead near mile 165.

163: Heartland

On your right is yet another school of higher education. While ISU holds rank as the oldest public state university in Illinois, Heartland Community College is 133 years its junior and is currently Illinois' youngest public two-year community college. With its youth comes new design for a "greener world." Heartland's Work Development Center, which opened in 2007, became the first state-funded building to receive the LEED (Leadership in Energy and Environmental Design) certification. From your car, you can see the glass walls and rooftops that reduce the need for artificial light. The building's temperature is controlled by 180 geothermal wells. It is composed of recycled building materials and houses energy-efficient machines. From the outdoor lights that face the ground to reduce light pollution to the interior sensors in bathrooms that reduce water waste, this building is an energy-efficient model for the future. The building fits right in this landscape with the nearby huge wind turbines that also offer alternative energy. You can read more about the energy wind farms produce at mile 216S.

164: Higher Ground

The wind turbines that you've just passed work to capture the wind, and what better place to catch a breeze than here at the highest elevation along Interstate 55. At mile 113, Elkhart Hill couldn't be ignored for its 700-foot elevation above the highway. But your car tires have slowly been climbing up the Bloomington Moraine, from the 500-foot highway elevation near Elkhart to just over 870 feet above sea level here.

Traveling through Illinois

168: Duncan Manor

The beautiful brick Italianate farmhouse ahead on the right has impressed travelers since 1875, when it was built alongside the Chicago & Alton Railroad. Livestock businessman William R. Duncan situated his majestic manor prominently on the hill near the rail lines so that Illinois travelers could admire his stately home. Read more at 171S about how Diane Sullivan was inspired to restore this historic home.

172: World's Window

Atop the white barn ahead on the right, a cupola rises from the shingles like a miniature house on a rooftop. If you were driving past ocean waves rather than waves of corn, you might see a woman peering from the windows of that cupola, waiting anxiously for the return of her lover from the sea. If you were in a village, you might see a bell in that cupola and the wooden barn sides transformed into a mighty cathedral. Cupolas have adorned medieval castles, European cathedrals, eastern temples and Greek and Roman ruins for centuries. This architectural feature is usually placed at the top of a roof or dome and gives structures a flare of romance—the cherry on top of the sundae. A cupola on a lighthouse is called a belvedere or "widow's walk," while a cupola that encases church bells is called a belfry. Even the National Aeronautics and Space Administration (NASA) is working on a space cupola so astronauts can get an exceptional view while they work.

In the United States, this ornamental structure was transformed into a beneficial architectural feature, and by the 1860s, many barns were using it. The barn cupola serves as a lantern and vent. Barn safety improved when farmers could rely on the cupola's natural light and use their oil lamps less often around the highly flammable hay. The vent in the cupola helps circulate air to keep hay dry and release excess heat to keep animals comfortable. You'll see cupolas in the many grain elevators and barns along I-55. In a grain elevator, the cupola is called the "head house," and it is where the elevated grain is directed into multiple storage bins. You may have also seen other cupolas today on structures like the Illinois capitol dome in Springfield and the St. Paul Lutheran Church at mile 30.

Northbound

178: Lexington

Lexington was established in 1836 by two men, Asahel Gridley (a colleague of Abraham Lincoln, a land investor and McLean County's first millionaire) and James Brown. It received its name because James Brown came from Lexington, Kentucky, and Gridley's father fought with the minutemen in the Battle of Lexington, Massachusetts, the first battle in the Revolutionary War. Those two factors made their town's name an obvious choice.

180: University Farm

The next generation of farmers tends the 360-acre farm ahead at mile 181 on your left. The Illinois State University farm offers hands-on training, research and outreach activities for its agricultural and agribusiness students. Located just eighteen miles northeast of campus, many students assist a small full-time staff in raising corn, soybeans, alfalfa, swine, beef and sheep. Compost created here is used throughout the community. Local companies bring their employees to the farm to teach them about everything from seeds to safety. Pioneer/DuPont and Mycogen/Dow experiment with new products. State Farm Insurance Company conducts safety audits here to train its employees. While most employees are students, this is a working farm that makes about $500,000 annually. Read more about this farm at 182S.

181: Wooded Islands

Notice in the fields that farmsteads are hidden behind stands of trees. When settlers first arrived, they found the prairies to be a sea of grasses virtually without trees. Today, corn and soybeans have replaced the grass, and trees are still scarce except where farmers have created these wooded islands in the cropland sea. Farmers plant rows of trees called farmstead windbreaks, or shelterbelts, on the north and west sides of their farms. Settlers planted trees because the treeless prairies seemed empty, and they missed the forests of their eastern homes. Today, farmers plant trees for protection from the winter winds and for shade during the hot summers. Trees planted around the farmstead provided many rural children with hours of entertainment playing in shady treehouses or on tire swings. Not only do they make life around the farm more comfortable, but by reducing the wind, they also reduce energy costs for

Traveling through Illinois

Trees help protect farmsteads from the prairie winds. *LuAnn Cadden.*

heating and cooling and they protect the exteriors of barns and homes from being stripped away by the elements. These shelterbelts can also be placed to reduce stress on livestock and prevent snow from piling up in the farmyard or on driveways. Over the next few miles, you will see many farmsteads located in the hearts of their own shady wooded islands.

185: From Cows to Cats

The pretty farmstead ahead on the left was originally a dairy farm built in 1900. The rare and unusual brown tile dairy barn has attracted professional photographers, and photos of it have been used in calendars and agricultural magazines. The Trachsel family lived here for many years beginning in the 1940s. When they lived here, it was a grain farm, as they grew corn and soybeans on 230 acres. You'll notice that even though there is an overpass here, there is no interstate pond. Mr. Trachsel refused to give up the additional acreage for a pond, so soil for the overpass was hauled in from other "interstate pond" excavation sites along the highway.

Northbound

Being so close to the highway meant serving travelers in need, especially in the days before cellphones. One New Year's Eve in the middle of an ice storm, a man showed up at their door saying that his car had slid into a ditch. He was on his way home to Pontiac after celebrating the holiday. He obviously had too much to drink. He asked if he could use the phone to call his wife to come get him. The Trachsels heard him say at his end, "Oh. Yeah. Okay." After hanging up, he said, "She told me that I have the car." Mr. Trachsel drove him home.

Today, Terrie McCarty owns the farmstead. Instead of farming, she runs a nonprofit called Happy Hearts Haven. She has converted the machine shed into a home for cats with feline leukemia and feline AIDS and uses the barn to house larger animals with special needs. Currently, three sheep, two horses, a goat and a potbellied pig are calling this haven home.

187: Livingston County, I Presume

Just ahead, you will enter Livingston County. Carved from LaSalle and McLean Counties in 1837, Livingston County was named after Edward Livingston, a prominent politician. He was mayor of New York City and represented New York and later Louisiana in Congress. He also served as Andrew Jackson's secretary of state, as a member of Jackson's staff at the Battle of New Orleans and as a minister to France. He had no connections to Illinois, but the Illinois General Assembly thought that he deserved to be honored by having a county named after him.

188: Down the Drain

The ditches crossing the surrounding fields just before mile 189 are critical to the farmers working this land. The flat Illinois cropland tends to collect and hold melting snow and rainfall. Farmers bury networks of tile drains to collect water from the soil and carry it into these ditches, where it flows away from fields. Removing water from soil with tile drainage allows fields to warm up faster in spring and be planted earlier. It lowers the water table and provides better aeration to plant roots. Moreover, draining the water through these underground systems reduces erosion from surface runoff. Farmers even use less energy and reduce wear and tear on their equipment when tilling dry, rather than muddy, soils. Tile drainage and these ditches may make the difference between profit and loss for Illinois farmers.

196: Pontiac

This town, like the former General Motors auto brand, is named for Chief Pontiac, a great Ottawa Indian leader. Early settler Jesse Fell named the post office Pontiac in honor of the distinguished chief and his own hometown of Pontiac, Michigan. Chief Pontiac organized tribes throughout the Great Lakes region to fight the British in what is known as Pontiac's War (1763–64). Eventually, Pontiac signed a peace treaty with the British in 1766. He was murdered by a Peoria Indian three years later. To avenge Pontiac's murder, the Ottawa Indians retaliated by killing many Peoria Indians.

199: Mount Trashmore

The mountainous peak rising more than 170 feet from the flat farmland on the left is Allied Waste's Livingston Landfill. Each day, 250 trucks bring in five thousand tons of trash from Bloomington-Normal and Chicago. This 461-acre landfill accepts millions of tons of waste each year, more waste than any other landfill in Illinois. Allied Waste hopes to create energy from the methane gas that is produced by the decomposing garbage. The company believes that it could produce enough to supply the electricity needs of a town the size of nearby Pontiac. If you are from Bloomington-Normal or the Chicago area, you may have contributed to the creation of this mountain of trash. Just think: you might be passing by some things that you threw out years ago.

200: Pontiac RV

Ahead on your right is a family-owned business that has been selling and servicing RVs for thirty years. Pontiac RV is the largest RV dealership in Illinois, and its fifteen-acre facility includes a showroom that displays more than one hundred vehicles. They have provided RVs for use by film crews filming movies in Chicago and supplied trailers to the Federal Emergency Management Administration (FEMA) in the aftermath of Hurricane Katrina. RVs often are donated for charitable events, including an episode of ABC-TV's *Extreme Makeover: Home Edition*. Like a turtle that carries its home on its back, RV enthusiasts take their homes with them in their travels. RV owners share a passion for the road. St. Augustine noted that "the world is a book, and those who do not travel read only a page." RVers are avid readers of the American landscape.

Northbound

203: Lofty "Grain"deur

Tall crop-filled silos, like the ones on your right, line this highway. Groups of silos usually indicate a grain elevator, simply a place where farmers take their crops to be stored, sold and transported. When Illinois' first farmers produced crops, they fed their families with them, sold a little of them and stored the rest on their farm. But as farming technology brought better plows, planting and harvesting tools, farmers produced crops faster and in greater volume than they could store on their farm. Once the grain elevator was invented in 1842, farmers had a place to store their high yields.

You'll see grain elevators lining the lanes of Interstate 55. Nearby market areas make it easy for a farmer to transport his grain by truck. After the grain is weighed, the farmer empties it into a receiving pit at the bottom of the grain elevator. The entire elevator is stacked like the Jolly Green Giant of grain sorting and storage. From the receiving pit, the grain is dumped into the "boot" of the elevator. Buckets on a vertical conveyor belt scoop up the grain in the "boot" and carry it up the "leg." At the top of the elevator, the grain enters the "head house," and from here, it is directed into selected bins and mixed with grain from other farms. At some point, this farmer's grain will be sold to a mill, where it will be processed into flours or oils, or sent on to be mixed with other ingredients to manufacture the toothpaste you use, the makeup you wear, the toys you buy for your children and the car that you're driving right now.

206: Wind Farm

Back at mile 70, you may recall seeing the one huge wind turbine towering over crops and supplying electricity for its neighbors. You may have also seen the wind turbines way off on your left near mile 133. Over the next few miles, you will get a close-up view of hundreds of immense turbines as they convert the breeze into electricity.

If you drive I-55 frequently, you've noticed how quickly the landscape from Dwight to Bloomington has changed since 2008. The once wide, empty sky is now cluttered by propellers near and far. Hundreds of wind turbines fill the skies of Livingston County. In the next few miles, you will see a wind farm owned by Iberdrola Renewables, LLC. This farm has 150 turbines and produces three hundred megawatts (capacity). As these enormous blades turn, they send electricity streaming through power lines to a grid used by the Tennessee Valley Authority.

Traveling through Illinois

A barn in the shadow of a wind farm. *Ted Cable.*

Wind farms provide clean energy, thousands of new jobs and a hefty pay check for landowners who allow companies to use their land. But others aren't so happy about the blades that cut through the sky in their backyard. Some landowners complain that the sound can go from a soft refrigerator-like hum to a roar that slashes through the walls of their home and keeps them awake at night. They also say that the huge shadows from the propellers are distracting and have even caused cases of vertigo. Crop-dusters say that it is dangerous for them to maneuver around the structures and through the different wind currents they create. It also makes it difficult for their crop chemicals to fall accurately on the fields. Read more about Illinois wind farms at 216S.

212: Barn Again

On the left side of the interstate, an old barn begins to show its age. In Illinois, less than one-third the number of barns that existed a hundred years ago remain. Traditional barns of yesteryear are not big enough to store modern tractors and combines and not hygienic enough for modern dairy

Northbound

Persevering on the prairie. *LuAnn Cadden.*

operations, and hay no longer needs a loft. Although many farm families have a sentimental attachment to their old wooden barns, maintenance can be expensive; so many barns fall into neglect and slowly succumb to nature and gravity. Since 1987, *Successful Farming* magazine and the National Trust for Historic Preservation have conducted a program called Barn Again! that encourages farmers to rehabilitate their historic barns. Each year, this program helps about seven hundred barn owners by offering demonstration projects, case studies, publications, technical assistance and an awards program. Some farmers convert their old barns into quaint stores, artist studios or even into bed-and-breakfast businesses. With some ingenuity, old barns can be put to new use.

216: Dwight

Like many towns along I-55, Dwight traces its roots to the railroad and to the "Mother Road," Route 66. When the first trains came through from Chicago to St. Louis in 1854, a water tank for the steam engines was built here. A small village sprung up and was named Dwight after Henry Dwight, a New Yorker who had heavily invested in building the railroad from Bloomington to Joliet. Later, Route 66 passed through the city. Ambler's Texaco Station, built in 1933, a relic of the Mother Road, is now a visitor's information center.

Dwight's history is strongly linked to social welfare efforts. Leslie Keeley founded the Keeley Institute here in 1879. It offered the "Keeley Cure," a secret commercial treatment for alcoholism. At one time, more than two hundred branches of the institute operated throughout the United States and Europe. By 1939, in response to Keeley's famous slogan, "Drunkenness is a disease and I can cure it," more than 400,000 people received injections of the Keeley Cure. At its peak in popularity, 800 people per week were arriving in Dwight by train to visit the institute in spite of skepticism by the mainstream medical profession. The institute closed in 1965.

Dwight Correctional Center, established in 1930, is a maximum-security prison for women. The Helping Paws program here teaches grooming techniques and service dog training strategies to the female prisoners that make it easier for them to work in the pet industry. Dwight's Guardian Angel Bassett Rescue Inc. pairs unwanted Bassett Hounds to caring owners. Each year, hundreds of Bassett Hounds and their proud owners from around the country join a downtown parade called the "Basset Waddle."

220: Delivering Groceries

The large building off to the right after the underpass is the ALDI Distribution Warehouse. ALDI is an international discount grocery chain with more than one thousand stores in thirty-one states in the Midwest and eastern United States. ALDI also has grocery stores throughout Europe and Australia. This particular warehouse employs about seventy-five people, making it one of Dwight's biggest employers.

222: Power to the People

The power lines crossing the highway ahead bring electricity all the way from the Kincaid Junction Power Plant south of Springfield. This might seem strange because in just a few miles you will be passing a huge nuclear power plant, but the electricity from that coal fired plant south of Springfield supplements the power produced at the nuclear power plant (and several other power plants) to meet the energy needs of people and industry in the Chicago area. It is cheaper to send the energy up here in the form of electricity than shipping the coal here to generate electricity locally. The power in these lines enters the power grid merging and mixes with electricity produced at the other plants to provide light and power to Chicagoland. Learn more about electricity's journey across the state at 224S.

226: Gardner

This town was named for Henry A. Gardner. Gardner was not only the chief engineer for the Chicago & Alton Railroad, but he also owned the land where this town's old train station was built in 1854.

227: Smooth Sumac

On the right, you will notice the tree-like smooth sumac shrub covering the hillside. Except in winter, you'll recognize it by its long, narrow leaflets that droop like palm leaves. This tree-like shrub's extensive root system is perfect for preventing erosion. Sumac produces dark-red velvety fruits that are eaten by more than thirty kinds of birds. Humans like it, too. The crushed fruit also produces a tart lemonade-like drink when mixed with water and sugar. Native Americans smoked the leaves, treated fever with the fruits and used the entire plant for staining and dyeing. You can't miss noticing sumac in the fall. Sumac leaves, when they turn a deep scarlet red, are the first to signal that fall has arrived.

230: Mud Dump

Locals call the high steep hill on the left a "mud dump." Mud dumps rise out of the flat landscape like small volcanoes. Nighttime travelers on I-55 have asked local gas station attendants how the "pyramids" got here. Though not as old as the pyramids, these mud dumps are well over one hundred years old. This mud dump was created in the 1880s. When excavating mine shafts and tunnels, miners piled the rocks and soil that they removed into these miniature mountains at the surface. Old-timers affectionately call them by the name or number of the mine from which they came. Because the material on the mounds is acidic, plants do not grow on them naturally. To prevent the acids from getting into surrounding farmland, government reclamation efforts have tried to plant alfalfa or grass on them by mixing seed, straw and "enough fertilizer to grow crops on a car hood" into the soil. Sometimes it worked, but often it didn't. Many mud dumps are removed entirely when the mined material is used for "fill" for construction projects. When mud dumps are hauled away, locals are sad to see these monuments to mining disappear from the land.

233: Movie Motel

For you movie buffs, you might recognize the Sun Motel on the right just after the overpass. This motel was used as the "Braidwood Inn" in filming the 1987 movie *Planes, Trains and Automobiles*, which starred Steve Martin and John Candy. Their characters, Neal and Del, finished the last leg of a grueling journey home to Chicago for Thanksgiving by driving I-55 from St Louis. This motel is famous for the scene where stranded travelers Neal and Del have to share a bed overnight in Wichita, Kansas. Chicago-native director John Hughes found this motel a little closer to home and filmed a memorable scene here over two or three days. The famous "pillows" scene took place here in room 114:

> *Neal: Del...Why did you kiss my ear?*
> *Del: Why are you holding my hand?*
> *Neal:* [frowns] *Where's your other hand?*
> *Del: Between two pillows...*
> *Neal: Those aren't pillows!*

Neal and Del also had their share of mishaps on Interstate 55:

> [They enter the highway on an exit ramp, and a driver frantically tries to alert them.]
> *Neal: He says we're going the wrong way...*
> *Del: Oh, he's drunk. How would he know where we're going?*

> [A state trooper pulls over their damaged rental car.]
> *State trooper: What are you driving here?*
> *Del: We had a small fire last night, but we caught it in the nick of time.*
> *State trooper: Do you have any idea how fast you were going?*

Northbound

The Sun Motel: Hollywood comes to Will County. *Ted Cable.*

Del: Funny enough, I was just talking to my friend about that. Our speedometer has melted, and as a result, it's hard to see with any degree of accuracy exactly how fast we were going.

Many travelers and even tour buses have stopped by the Sun Motel to see the infamous room where Neal and Del spent the night. For those movie buffs with an eye for detail, you may notice that the scenes filmed just outside the hotel show a coal mine hill on the other side of I-55. That hill has since been removed, but the Sun Motel still welcomes travelers on their way to and from Chicago. We hope your journey to the Chicago area has been much smoother than it was for Neal and Del!

235: Take a Gander at the Geese

As you approach the Des Plaines Conservation Area at mile 241, on your left, and as you continue through the Chicago suburbs ahead, you may see flocks of Canada geese in the ponds or fields. Yes, that's right. They are officially called "Canada geese," not the more widely used "Canadian geese." To many people, the honking of a V-formation of geese flying high overhead represents wilderness on the wing; to others, migrating geese signal the changing of the seasons. However, in urban areas, Canada geese often conjure up less romantic notions of a noisy nuisance and goose droppings under your feet.

Canada geese are vegetarians. They can be found in croplands eating grain, but they especially love to graze on young shoots of grasses. This is why they congregate on lawns and golf courses, especially if a pond is nearby where they can loaf when not eating. These situations prompt a love-hate relationship between geese and humans. Although people generally like seeing and even feeding these entertaining birds and their fuzzy goslings, these feathered families leave behind a mess. Their droppings can pollute ponds and foul golf course greens, swimming beaches, residential sidewalks and lawns in housing developments with ponds. Each Canada goose produces 1.5 pounds of droppings per day. Five million resident (nonmigrating) Canada geese live in the continental United States. Five million times 1.5 pounds per day is a lot of poop! An entire industry has developed to deal with ridding airports, neighborhoods and golf courses of geese. Strategies used include tethered kites that look like swooping eagles, trained dogs and trapping and relocation. A preventive approach is to design ponds with steep banks with tall grass, as geese prefer mowed areas.

It's hard to believe that these amazing creatures were almost extinct due to overhunting and habitat loss in the early twentieth century. The giant Canada goose subspecies (the one often seen along I-55) was believed to be extinct until 1962, when a small flock was discovered in Minnesota. These wide-bodied flyers can weigh more than twenty pounds and have a nearly six-foot wingspan. When migrating, they can fly as high as eight thousand feet and cover several hundred miles during a day. Canada geese mate for life at the age of two and have young at age three. Love 'em or hate 'em, wild or tame, we now share our urban landscapes with these winged wonders.

238: I&M Canal

Just ahead, you will see a sign that you are entering the historic I&M Canal Heritage Corridor. This canal opened in 1848, finally completing the continuous water route from the Atlantic Ocean to the Gulf of Mexico. Streams of commerce floated to Chicago on the canal from both the East

Loading grain along the Illinois & Michigan Canal. *Howard and Lois Adelmann Regional History Collection at Lewis University.*

and the South. Grain, limestone, coal, salt and lumber were shipped back east inexpensively. Goods such as sugar, molasses, tobacco and oranges arrived from the South. Chicago developed into a major city and the entire region prospered because of this canal.

You will cross the canal about ten miles ahead near mile 249. Read more about the I&M transportation corridor at 250S.

241: Grant's Creek Nature Preserve

On the right, you can see a glimpse of native prairie protected in the Grant's Creek Nature Preserve. This moist, seventy-eight-acre prairie contains two to three feet of deep black prairie soil, which supports 110 different native plant species. It is home to many types of prairie reptiles, amphibians, mammals and birds. This is small remnant of the great Illinois prairies that existed prior to European settlement. Through pioneers' journals, we can

Traveling through Illinois

glimpse what the land looked like before paved roads began to divide it. In 1840, pioneer Eliza Steele wrote of the prairie near Joliet (mile 248, ahead) in her journal *Summer Journey in the West*:

> *I started with surprise and delight. I was in the midst of a prairie! A world of grass and flowers stretched around me, rising and falling in gentle undulations, as if an enchanter had struck the ocean swell, and it was at rest forever. We passed whole acres of blossoms, a carpet of every color intermixed, or narrow bands, as if a rainbow had fallen upon the verdant slopes. When the sun flooded this mosaic floor with light, and the summer breeze stirred among their leaves, the iridescent glow was beautiful and wondrous beyond anything I had ever conceived.*

244: ExxonMobil Refinery

Each day, this refinery on the right receives up to 250,000 barrels of crude oil piped down from Canada and turns them into 9 million gallons of gasoline and diesel fuel. That's enough to drive your car around the world more than seven thousand times! About 90 percent of what comes out of a barrel of Canadian crude refined here is gasoline and diesel, but propane, butane and asphalt also are distilled from the crude oil. Nothing goes to waste here. Some byproducts are even used in steel mills, cement production and power generation. This refinery runs twenty-four hours a day, 365 days a year, with a workforce of more than six hundred people, to provide energy for our homes, industries and cars that cruise along Interstate 55.

245: War and Peace

Arsenal Road (exit 245) is named for the Joliet Army Ammunition Plant, formerly called the Joliet Arsenal, where the U.S. Army made and packaged more than 4 billion pounds of explosives. This plant was established in 1940 and covered almost thirty-seven thousand acres. During World War II, it was the largest and most advanced ammunition plant in the world, employing more than ten thousand people and making more than 926 million bombs, shells, mines, detonators and fuses, as well as more than 1 billion pounds of TNT. Other activities included testing ammunition, washout and renovation of shells and demolition of explosives. The plant

Northbound

Abraham Lincoln National Cemetery. *Ted Cable.*

was reactivated during the Korean and Vietnam Wars, but by the 1970s, production wound down.

Since 1996, this land has been used for peaceful purposes. The U.S. Army transferred 19,165 acres of this land to the U.S. Forest Service and created the Midewin National Tallgrass Prairie, the first national tallgrass prairie in the United States (exit 241). Today, 7,200 acres of this tranquil prairie are open to the public for enjoying nature. Interestingly, 392 "igloos" (which stored ammunition) remain on the property. They were built to withstand the explosion of their highly volatile contents, and therefore they cost too much to dismantle. These structures, which once stored TNT, are now used to store prairie plants and seeds. In 1999, a quiet peace spread over another 982 acres of the old arsenal when the Department of Veterans Affairs established the Abraham Lincoln National Cemetery. This cemetery provides 400,000 burial spaces for veterans and their families. War veterans now rest where bombs and bullets were brought into the world. It is fitting that it is named after Lincoln because during the Civil War, President Lincoln signed the law that established national cemeteries for veterans.

TRAVELING THROUGH ILLINOIS

248: World's First Dairy Queen

On June 22, 1940, the world's first Dairy Queen opened here in Joliet and sold soft-serve cones for five cents. Two years earlier, J.F. McCullough had invented soft serve because he thought hard ice cream, served at zero degrees Fahrenheit, "froze your taste buds." He figured out a way to serve the smooth soft serve at a more comfortable twenty-two degrees Fahrenheit and asked a friend to sell it at his ice cream store in Kankakee, Illinois. Soft serve was so popular that McCullough and his friend opened the first of what are now 5,845 Dairy Queen locations in twenty countries. You can still get a soft-serve cone or even a Double Fudge Cookie Dough Blizzard in Joliet, but not at the original location. The original building still exists and is protected by a historic designation, but it is now home to the Universal Church of the Kingdom of God. Read at 254S about how Joliet was named.

250: Coast-to-Coast Highways

You will be crossing two coast-to-coast highways, each built in a different era of highway travel. First, you'll encounter Interstate 80, built in the 1960s and early 1970s, and then US 30 (the Lincoln Highway), built in the 1920s and 1930s (mile 257). Read more at 252S about these two roads that parallel each other and become the same highway in stretches as they cross North America.

251: Heating Up Chicago

If you have a gas oven or furnace and you live in the Chicago area, there is a good chance that the gas that heats your food or warms your home passes through the natural gas facility to your right. These mysterious-looking pipes going into and out of the ground are a compression station for the largest transporter of natural gas into the Chicago area and one of the largest gas transport companies in the world. The natural gas that arrives here comes from the bottom of the Gulf of Mexico and gas fields of west Texas and New Mexico. It travels through National Gas Pipeline Company's system of 9,800 miles of pipelines to bring it to your house. We sometimes forget that beneath the ground a maze of pipelines moves water, oil and gas great distances, mingling with the phone lines and other communication cables that transport data beneath our feet. A lot is going on down there! This compression station adds the pressure necessary to push the natural gas through pipes to the customers. To meet peak demand, National Gas Pipeline Company can provide the Chicago area with nearly 5 billion cubic feet of natural gas per day—all to provide warmth for Chicagoans.

253: Where There's a Will, There's a (High) Way

The story of Will County is a dynamic tale of people on the move. For hundreds of years, the Des Plaines, Illinois and Kankakee Rivers were highways for Native Americans, explorers, trappers and settlers moving through what is now Will County. Construction of the I&M Canal brought Irish immigrants in the early 1800s. Coal mining and limestone quarrying brought thousands of people here in the mid- to late 1800s. Another wave of people moved into the area during World War II to work in war-related industries. After the war, the interstate system crisscrossed Will County, providing a new set of highways: I-57, I-80 (just ahead) and, of course, I-55. People are still on the move here. Will County's population is expected to double from 600,000 to more than 1.2 million over the next twenty-five years. It is the fastest-growing county in Illinois and the tenth-fastest growing county in the United States. Considering the many people who passed through Will County, it is surprising that the county is named for Dr. Conrad Will, a southern Illinois legislator and member of the first Illinois Constitutional Convention, who never lived or worked near here.

256: The Lincoln Highway

At exit 257, you will cross US 30, better known as Lincoln Highway. Lincoln Highway was the first road to go from coast to coast, originally starting in Times Square in New York City and ending 3,389 miles later in Lincoln Park in San Francisco. It was dedicated in 1913, nine years before the Lincoln Memorial in Washington, D.C., making it the first national memorial to Abraham Lincoln. The idea for the highway came at an Indianapolis dinner party in 1912. Carl Fischer, who helped start the Indianapolis 500, hosted a group of wealthy men who were interested in the fledgling auto industry. Over dinner, he convinced them that for their auto industry to grow, people would need good roads. By the end of the evening, the men had pledged several hundred thousand dollars to establish the Lincoln Highway.

In 1923, just east of here near the Indiana state line, a 1.3-mile stretch of Lincoln Highway was built as a national model for modern road construction. This "Ideal Section" featured ten-inch-thick reinforced concrete, two lanes in each direction, hidden drainage, landscaping and lighting—the last two of which being rare along roads in those days. In 1926, the new U.S. Numbered Highway System designated most of the Lincoln Highway as US 30. Today, US 30 runs from Atlantic City, New Jersey, to Astoria, Oregon. Much like the railroads before them, U.S. highways brought prosperity to villages and towns located along the route. As you travel I-55, consider how we take highway travel for granted and how far highway travel has come in the last one hundred years.

262: Big Box Boom

Over the next few miles, the highway is lined with single-story distribution facilities. As you drive among semis, you are witnessing the story of the transportation of goods from producers to markets. One key element of that story is the need for warehouses and distribution centers within complex supply chains. On the outskirts of the third-largest city in the country, almost two hundred warehouses receive thousands of shipments from around the world. Enormous amounts of manufactured goods must be stored temporarily before being strategically and efficiently sent on their way to retail outlets, where we purchase the products. Some of these distribution centers fulfill more than five hundred orders per day. Efficient distribution lowers the price of the goods we purchase. These "big boxes" have had a recent boom along the Stevenson Expressway (mile 277). Between 1999 and 2009, distribution centers along the Stevenson grew from 12 to 193. Not only are these centers perfectly poised on Chicago's border, between an interstate to the west and a shipping canal and railroad to the east, but they are also just inside the border of Will County, which allows them to pay lower tax rates.

265: Quantum Foods

The impressive building on the right is the corporate headquarters of Quantum Foods, one of the world's leading suppliers of beef, pork and poultry products, as well as of custom menu items to restaurant chains, the military and school foodservice facilities. It also partners with retailers on prepared meals and deli products. Quantum's research and development team creates unique flavors and portions for specific customer needs. Quantum's products are either fully cooked or ready-to-cook meals, including such diverse products as chicken fried steak, fajitas, bacon-wrapped filets, kabobs, meatballs, spare ribs, several smoked meats and breaded meat products and meat in sauces such as pot roasts. The next time you eat in a restaurant, there is a good chance that your menu item will have been developed right here at Quantum Foods and then sent from here to your restaurant's kitchen. Quantum serves thirty of the top fifty restaurant chains, as well as companies in more than fifteen countries.

267: LaGROU

Another impressive facility along here is the LaGROU warehouse. And warehouses are its business! Many of these warehouses belong to a specific manufacturing company to store its products, but LaGROU offers regional and national distribution services from its network of nine strategically located warehouse facilities, one of which you see here on the right. It handles storing and managing inventory, as well as shipment of all sorts of products, especially food and beverage products, because its warehouses include refrigerated and freezer space. LaGROU is noteworthy for having served more than 20 million people at the annual Taste of Chicago Festival. It has provided all of the onsite food and beverage logistics and refrigeration since the beginning of this festival more than twenty-five years ago.

269: DuPage County

As you pass through the I-355/I-55 intersection, you enter DuPage County. Almost 1 million people live in DuPage County, making it the second most populated county in Illinois next to Cook County, which you will enter soon.

272: Almost There!

A brown Route 66 sign here reminds you that you are still driving along the "Mother Road." Decades ago, travelers such as you still felt the same sensation near the end of their journey, whether long or short. Imagine the travelers who had ventured all the way from Los Angeles as they were approaching the route's terminus.

274: Suburban Signals

Water towers rising above the flat urban landscape signal that you have entered the Chicago suburbs. The towers on the left supply water to Willowbrook. At 275S, read more about the benefits of having a water tower in your community.

275: Skyline Song

Way off in the distance, downtown Chicago rises up to say, "Hello!" Whether you're returning home, visiting again or have never set foot or wheel on Lake Shore Drive, the skyline calls with its bluesy voice just the same: "Come on, baby. Don't you want to go? Back to that same 'ole place, Sweet Home Chicago." If the skyline looks unfamiliar, it is because you are seeing the backside of the iconic Chicago skyline. Virtually all photos of downtown Chicago feature skyscrapers rising above Lake Michigan and the expansive lakefront parks. You will be entering downtown Chicago's backdoor.

Chicago's skyline as seen from the west. Collectively, Chicago skyscrapers create the world's tallest skyline. *Ted Cable.*

Northbound

276: Crowded County

Just ahead, you'll enter Cook County, the second most populated county in the United States. Only Los Angeles County has more people. You are now in the heart of Chicagoland and are surrounded by almost 10 million people spread over Cook and several other counties. If you are just visiting the city, you are one of 32.4 million domestic leisure travelers, 11.7 million domestic business travelers or 1.3 million overseas visitors who come to Chicago each year.

277: The Stevenson

As you cross into Cook County, I-55 becomes the Stevenson Expressway. These final eighteen miles of I-55 are named for Adlai Stevenson II. Stevenson was a former governor of Illinois who twice ran unsuccessfully for president against Dwight Eisenhower. Stevenson also lost to John F. Kennedy in the Democratic primaries leading up to the 1960 election, but Kennedy later appointed him to serve as ambassador to the United Nations.

The interstate system around Chicago radiates out from the city like spokes on a tire. This "spoke" leads from the southwestern suburbs and neighborhoods into downtown. In fact, when this stretch of I-55 opened in 1964, it was called the Southwest Expressway. In a speech at a Democratic National Convention, this highway's namesake famously encouraged Americans to demonstrate "sacrifice, patience, understanding, and implacable purpose." These characteristics are required when driving the Stevenson. The Texas Transportation Institute named these northbound lanes of I-55 between IL-53 and IL-83 and between Harlem and County Line Road (ahead) as some of the most frustrating commutes in the nation. Although it is often congested, it is the unpredictable nature of the traffic that landed this highway on the list of most difficult commutes. Drivers not wanting to be late need to allow themselves two and a half times the normal travel time due to the uncertainty of the traffic congestion. For example, the worst nine-mile stretch may take nine minutes or almost half an hour. To promote efficiency, public transit buses on the Stevenson are allowed to drive on the shoulders.

Traveling through Illinois

Approaching Chicago

As you enter Chicago, we will discontinue using mile markers for stories so that you are not distracted by looking for signs and can better focus on the exceedingly busy highway. A parade of bumper-to-bumper cars can halt at a moment's notice and leave you nestled in the back seat of the car in front of you if you're not careful. So, although we'll continue to share stories, we hope that the driver focuses first and foremost on the road before locating objects along the roadside.

Here on Chicago's southwest side, the interstate is surrounded by railroad lines, crisscrossing waterways and airplanes above. Being located on Lake Michigan shore, Chicago was ideally situated to become a transportation and commerce center. In 1848, the Illinois & Michigan (I&M) Canal, which you crossed at mile 238, linked the Great Lakes with the Mississippi River. East–west rail lines and later highways curved around Lake Michigan and crisscrossed the Chicago area. Even today, half of the nation's railroad freight passes through Chicago. And the combined air traffic at nearby Midway and O'Hare Airports makes Chicago the busiest aviation center.

Near mile 279, you'll again cross over the Des Plaines River. If you visit the Loop and cross a downtown bridge over the Chicago River, you'll cross over waters that end up here in the Des Plaines River. Just before Harlem Avenue (282) you'll pass over the Chicago Sanitary and Ship Canal, which replaced the I&M Canal in 1900. The canal empties Chicago of its treated sewage and supports commerce-driven barge traffic—thereby reducing the interstate's semi-trailer congestion. Products and people are being transported all around you by these river highways and in and out of Midway Airport, located on Cicero Avenue (exit 286).

At Cicero Avenue, you will officially enter the city of Chicago. Chicago's western boundary is irregular to bring in Midway and O'Hare Airports. Surprisingly, there is no sign welcoming you or even an indication that you have entered this fine city. So let us be the first to welcome you to Chicago!

Just one mile after officially entering Chicago, you will be able to read its skyline. Just as St. Louis's arch anchors the south end of this journey, the black and boxy Willis Tower (formerly Sears Tower) dominates the skyline and anchors the northern terminus of I-55. Even without the antenna, at 1,450 feet and 110 stories high, Willis Tower is the third-tallest building in the world and the tallest building not just in the nation but also in the entire Western Hemisphere. If you include its antenna, the Willis Tower rises to 1,730 feet. This iconic building includes twenty-five thousand miles

NORTHBOUND

The Willis Tower soars 1,730 feet above the streets of Chicago. *Fleishman-Hillard.*

of plumbing and two thousand miles of electrical wire. It was built to sway in the Windy City's blasts, and it indeed moves several feet on an especially windy day. It has been featured in many movies, including *Ferris Bueller's Day Off* and *The Dark Knight*.

Traveling through Illinois

Willis, a London-based insurance firm, gained the naming rights in 2009. However, proud tradition-loving Chicagoans still call it Sears Tower, and if somebody refers to it as Willis Tower, they may mockingly offer up the 1980s catchphrase from the *Diff'rent Strokes* television show, "What you talkin' about, Willis?" The naming rights expire in 2024, so maybe its name will change again. Collectively, the skyscrapers ahead of you cooperate to create the world's tallest skyline. The four tallest buildings in the skyline are four of the six tallest skyscrapers in the United States, including the tallest (Willis Tower) and second-tallest (Trump Tower) buildings in North America. Illinois poet Carl Sandburg revealed the soul of skyscrapers in his poetry:

> *By day the skyscraper looms in the smoke and sun and has a soul.*
> *Prairie and valley, streets of the city, pour people into it and they mingle among its twenty floors and are poured out again back to the streets, prairies and valleys.*
> *It is the men and women, boys and girls so poured in and out all day that give the building a soul of dreams and thoughts and memories...*
> *Ten-dollar-a-week stenographers take letters from corporation officers, lawyers, efficiency engineers, and tons of letters go bundled from the building to all ends of the earth.*
> *Smiles and tears of each office girl go into the soul of the building just the same as the master-men who rule the building.*
> *Hands of clocks turn to noon hours and each floor empties its men and women who go away and eat and come back to work.*
> *Toward the end of the afternoon all work slackens and all jobs go slower as the people feel day closing on them.*
> *One by one the floors are emptied...*
> *By night the skyscraper looms in the smoke and the stars and has a soul.*

Pulaski Road (287) is another indication of Chicago's ethnic diversity and heritage. Chicago has the largest Polish population of any city outside of

Northbound

Poland. Every March, Chicago celebrates Casimir Pulaski Day, and schools and government offices close in honor of this Polish military leader who became an American Revolutionary War general. You will cross over Western Avenue just past mile 290. Western Avenue, Chicago's longest continuous street, marks what was once Chicago's western boundary. At 24.5 miles in length, it is one of the longest urban streets in the world.

Rather than a melting pot, Chicago is more like a colorful quilt consisting of seventy-seven distinct neighborhoods, including Greek Town, Little Italy, Little Seoul, Chinatown, Swedish Andersonville and several Hispanic, Lithuanian and Polish neighborhoods.

Ahead at the busy junction of I-94 and I-90 (292), you will see Chinatown on the right. Chicago's Chinatown is the fourth largest in the United States with fifteen thousand Chinese residents and scores of Chinese restaurants and other businesses.

Just past Chinatown, near mile 293, the Bronzeville neighborhood will be on your right. It has been home to African Americans since the "Great Migration" brought them here from the South for jobs in the twentieth century. Many jazz and blues musicians have called Bronzeville home, including Louis Armstrong, Muddy Waters, Buddy Guy, Willie Dixon and Lou Rawls.

End of the Road

At McCormick Place, Chicago's primary venue for trade shows and conventions, I-55 will deposit you on the famous Lake Shore Drive running alongside beautiful Lake Michigan, the Great Lake that kisses the city's edge with the romance of an ocean.

We encourage you to look beyond the spaceship-like Soldiers Field and ponder the iconic Chicago skyline. (Follow the signs to the Adler Planetarium and park there for a great view.) Nourished by water, forged by fire and built on soggy earth, this Windy City rose from the ashes like a phoenix and is now the third-largest city in the country. Chicago was destroyed by the Great Chicago Fire of 1871. The fire was particularly damaging because virtually all of the buildings and even sidewalks were made of wood. The near total devastation provided a unique opportunity for world-renowned architects such as Louis Sullivan to build a city from scratch. Chicago was rebuilt bigger and more uniquely American than any other city in the country. The

Traveling through Illinois

first steel-framed skyscrapers rose from the ashes, many of which are still considered to be architectural masterpieces. The debris from the fire was used to fill in along the Lake Michigan shoreline (which at the time was near present-day Michigan Avenue), creating land for what is now the Museum Campus and Grant and Millennium Parks. Architect Daniel Burnham, famous for saying, "Make no little plans; they have no magic to stir men's blood," designed Chicago's renowned lakefront parks on the debris. The parks, along with their backdrop of towering skyscrapers, still create magic to stir us.

We hope that this book helped stir in you interest and inspiration as we attempted to reveal the beauty of Illinois and the resourcefulness and productivity of its people. Thank you for traveling with us.

BIBLIOGRAPHY

Abraham Lincoln's Classroom. www.abrahamlincolnsclassroom.org/library.
Abraham Lincoln Tourism Bureau of Logan County. www.abe66.com.
Air Tractor. www.airtractor.com.
Alton Weekly Telegraph. "Ancient Landmarks—Meeting of Old Settlers of Madison County, Illinois: Who Were There, What They Said and What They Propose to Do." October 22, 1874. Madison County, Illinois GenWeb. http://madison.illinoisgenweb.org/reminiscences.html.
American Experience. "Chicago: City of the Century." PBS. www.pbs.org/wgbh/amex/chicago/filmmore/ps_fire.html.
American Wind Energy Association. www.awea.org/learnabout/publications/loader.cfm?csModule=security/getfile&PageID=6388.
Arch Coal Inc. www.archcoal.com.
The Ariston Café. www.ariston-cafe.com.
Arnold Transit Company. arnoldline.com.
Bakke, Dave. "Illinois Postcard: Elkhart Seems to Draw People In." *State Journal-Register*, October 24, 2009. www.sj-r.com/features/x23521522/Elkharts-colorful-history-continues-to-attract-attention.
The Barn Journal. "Efficiency of the Round Barn." www.thebarnjournal.org/round/efficiency.html.
Biodiesel Magazine. "ISA Soy 2020 Meeting Highlights Ill. Biodiesel Industry Growth." November 21, 2010. www.biodieselmagazine.com/articles/8174/isa-soy-2020-meeting-highlights-ill-biodiesel-industry-growth.

BIBLIOGRAPHY

Bogan, Jesse. "Fairmont City Facing a Future Without Its Landfill Revenue." *St. Louis Post-Dispatch*, February 28, 2012. www.stltoday.com/news/local/illinois/fairmont-city-facing-a-future-without-its-landfill-revenue/article_26865808-ee48-5eb1-a929-bdb716f6af41.html#ixzz1uabvr7zC.

Brain, Marshall. "How Water Towers Work." How Stuff Works. www.howstuffworks.com/water.htm.

Cable, Ted, and LuAnn Cadden. *Driving Across Missouri: A Guide to I-70*. Lawrence: University Press of Kansas, 2010.

Cable, Ted, and Wayne Maley. *Driving Across Kansas: A Guide to I-70*. Lawrence: University Press of Kansas, 2003.

Cahokia Mounds State Historic Site. www.cahokiamounds.org.

Callary, Edward. *Place Names of Illinois*. Urbana: University of Illinois Press, 2009.

Canal Corridor Association. www.canalcor.org.

Cargill. "Cargill Partners with Communities to Turn Waste into Energy." www.cargill.com/connections/more-stories/waste-into-energy/index.jsp.

———. "Innovation Train: How Cargill Moved 400,000 Bushels of Corn 1,300 Miles and Reinvented an Industry." www.cargill.com/connections/more-stories/innovation-train/index.jsp.

Choose Chicago. www.choosechicago.com.

City Barbs Blog. "Henry Ford and His Amazing Soybean Suit." January 11, 2007. www.citybarbs.com/2007/01/11/henry-ford-his-amazing-soybean-suit.

City, Water, Light and Power. "Dallman 4 Power Station." www.cwlp.com/electric_division/generation/Dallman_4.htm.

Clean Energy Authority. "What Is a Megawatt and a Megawatt-Hour?" www.cleanenergyauthority.com/solar-energy-resources/what-is-a-megawatt-and-a-megawatt-hour.

Cloud Appreciation Society. www.cloudappreciationsociety.org.

Coffey, Timothy. *The History and Folklore of North American Wildflowers*. Boston: Houghton Mifflin Company, 1993.

Corfidi, Stephen F. "The Colors of Sunset and Twilight." National Weather Service Storm Prediction Center, March 1996. www.spc.noaa.gov/publications/corfidi/sunset/?from=search_webresults%3C1%3E.

Cornell University Department of Natural Resources, Ecology and Management of Invasive Plants Program. "Phragmites: Common Reed." www.invasiveplants.net/phragmites/Default.htm.

Cupboard Wagon Inc. www.cupboardwagon.com/conestogawagon.html.

Cupola Consulting. www.cupola.com.

BIBLIOGRAPHY

Dale Coyne Racing. www.dalecoyneracing.com.
De Guzman, Doris. "The Use and Development of Renewable Chemicals in Automotive Parts Is Rising." ICIS, June 2, 2010. www.icis.com/Articles/2010/06/07/9364336/use-of-bio-based-auto-parts-is-increasing.html.
Dominion. "Kincaid Power Station." www.dom.com/about/stations/fossil/kincaid-power-station.jsp.
Duncan Manor. www.duncanmanor.org.
Elkhart Grain. www.elkhartgrain.com.
Exelon Corporation. www.exeloncorp.com.
Explore PA History. "Conestoga Wagon Historical Marker." www.explorepahistory.com/hmarker.php?markerId=1-A-60.
Federal Highway Administration, U.S. Department of Transportation. "Frequently Asked Questions." http://ops.fhwa.dot.gov/weather/faq.htm.
Federal Writers' Project of the Work Projects Administration for the State of Illinois. *Illinois: A Descriptive and Historical Guide*. Chicago: A.C. McClurg & Company, 1939.
Feeley, Thomas J., et al. *Department of Energy/Office of Fossil Energy's Power Plant Water Management R&D Program*. July 2005. www.netl.doe.gov/technologies/coalpower/ewr/pubs/IEP_Power_Plant_Water_R%26D_Final_1.pdf.
Finding Lincoln, Illinois. www.findinglincolnillinois.com.
Ford, Mary Ann. "Historic Towanda House on Endangered List." *Pantagraph*, March 1, 2007. www.pantagraph.com/news/article_04d798e2-ae9a-5ad3-a299-57c289e4ccbf.html.
Funks Grove Pure Maple Sirup. www.funkspuremaplesirup.com.
Funk, Stephen C. "The Irish Workers at Funks Grove." *Irish Immigrants in McLean County, Illinois*. Edited by Greg Koos. Bloomington, IL: McLean County Museum of History, 2000.
Furry, William. "Barely a Trace: What's Left of the Old Indian Trail Known as Edwards Trace." *Illinois Times*, October 4, 2001.
Garden Digest. "Trees." www.gardendigest.com/trees.htm.
Garvert, Melinda, Curtis Mann and Edward Russo. *Springfield Community Service: A Pictorial History*. St. Louis, MO: G. Bradley Publishing Inc., 1998.
Genealogy Trails. "Native Americans of Illinois" www.genealogytrails.com/ill/nativeamericans.html.
Glendinning, Gene V. *The Chicago & Alton Railroad: The Only Way*. DeKalb: Northern Illinois University Press, 2002. www.niupress.niu.edu/niupress/scripts/Book/bookresults.asp?ID=393.

Bibliography

Global Security. "Joliet Army Ammunition Plant." www.globalsecurity.org/military/facility/aap-joliet.htm.

GoodLogo! www.goodlogo.com/extended.info/2440

Graphic Design Blog. "25 Logos With Hidden Messages—Amazing Graphic Designing Tricks!" April 21, 2009. www.graphicdesignblog.org/hidden-logos-in-graphic-designing.

Grundy County, Illinois GenWeb. www.grundycountyil.org.

Hansel, A.K. "End Moraines: The End of the Glacial Ride." Illinois State Geological Survey, updated April 19, 2010. www.isgs.illinois.edu/maps-data-pub/publications/geobits/geobit2.shtml.

Hanson, Henry M. "Highway Plan Stirs Downstate Feud." *Chicago Daily News*, September 27, 1965.

Happy Hearts Haven. www.happyheartshaven.org.

Harper, Suzanne. *From Mare's Tails to Thunderheads: Clouds*. New York: Franklin Watts, 1997.

Henderson, Harold. "The Rise and Fall of the Mound People." *Chicago Reader*, June 29, 2000. www.chicagoreader.com/chicago/the-rise-and-fall-of-the-mound-people/Content?oid=902673.

Hinton, Wayne. "Coal and Coal Mining in Central Illinois." Wayne's World of History and Genealogy. www.gillespieil.com/ilcoalmines.html.

Historical Society of Montgomery County Illinois. www.history.montgomeryco.com.

Historic National Road. "Maps and Directions." www.nationalroadpa.org/maps_directions.html.

Holliday, Bob. "Route 66 Landmark Palms Grill Reopens in Atlanta." *Pantagraph*, May 19, 2009. www.pantagraph.com/business/article_85754d2a-e0eb-5dfd-9f55-51025eec23ab.html.

Howard, Robert P. "A New Eden: The Pioneer Era in Sangamon County." *Illinois: A History of the Prairie State*. Springfield, IL. Sangamon County Historical Society, 1974.

Hymowitz, Theodore. "Soybeans: The Success Story." National Soybean Research Laboratory. www.nsrl.uiuc.edu/aboutsoy/Success.pdf.

Illinois Central Historical Society. "A Brief Historical Sketch of the Illinois Central Railroad." www.icrrhistorical.org/icrr.history.html.

Illinois Coal Association. www.ilcoalassn.com.

Illinois Corn. www.ilcorn.org.

Illinois Department of Commerce & Economic Opportunity. "Coal." www.commerce.state.il.us/dceo/Bureaus/Coal.

Bibliography

Illinois Department of Natural Resources. "Division of Oil and Gas." www.dnr.state.il.us/mines/dog/index.htm.

Illinois Department of Transportation. www.dot.state.il.us.

———. "Getting Around Illinois." www.gettingaroundillinois.com.

Illinois General Assembly. Illinois Compiled Statutes, Highway Advertising Control Act 225 ILCS 440/6.03. www.ilga.gov/legislation/98/HB/09800HB2595.htm.

Illinois.gov. "Lt. Gov. Quinn Leads Ceremony Celebrating New Paul Simon Parkway." Illinois Government News Network, June 30, 2006. www3.illinois.gov/PressReleases/ShowPressRelease.cfm?SubjectID=14&RecNum=5038.

Illinois Highways. "Naming the Trails." August 1915. Windy City Road Warrior. http://www.windycityroadwarrior.com/Stories/IL_Hgwys_1915-08.pdf.

Illinois Pork Producers Association. www.ilpork.com.

Illinois Rivers Decision Support System. www.ilrdss.sws.uiuc.edu/links/rivers.asp?ri=6.

Illinois Route 66. www.illinoisroute66.org.

Illinois Soybean Association. www.ilsoy.org.

———. "Soy Biodiesel." http://www.ilsoy.org/isa/industrial-uses/biodiesel.

Illinois State Historical Society. www.historyillinois.org.

Illinois Statehouse. www.ilstatehouse.com.

Illinois State Museum. "American Bottom Landing." www.museum.state.il.us/RiverWeb/landings/Ambot.

———. "Illinois State Symbols." www.museum.state.il.us/exhibits/symbols.

———. "Mazon Creek Fossils." www.museum.state.il.us/exhibits/mazon_creek.

Illinois Wesleyan University. www.iwu.edu/aboutiwu.

Illinois Wildflowers. www.illinoiswildflowers.info/index.htm.

Illinois Wind Energy Coalition. www.windforillinois.org.

Illinois Windmills. www.illinoiswindmills.org/index_files/windfarms.htm.

Ingle, Paul. "End of the Road: After 75 years Dixie Truckers Home Closes the Book on Route 66." *Illinois Times*, September 25, 2003. www.illinoistimes.com/Springfield/article-501-end-of-the-road.html.

IOI Loders Croklaan Americas. www.northamerica.croklaan.com.

J.H. Hawes Grain Elevator Museum. www.haweselevator.org.

Jacobshagen, Keith. "Personal Journey." *The Changing Prairie*. Edited by A. Joern and K.H. Keeler. New York: Oxford University Press, 1995.

Kamin, Blair. "Chicago, that Shape-Shifting Town: 'Chicago From the Sky' Captures 25 Years of Dramatic Transformation, with a Few Exceptions." *Chicago Tribune*, April 21, 2011, section 3, LIVE!, 3.

Bibliography

Kanfer, Larry. *Barns of Illinois*. Champaign: University of Illinois Press, 2009.
Kemp, Bill. "Kids Gathered Milkweed Pods for WWII Effort." *Pantagraph*, October 13, 2007. www.pantagraph.com/news/article_5099b3d3-117e-52c6-8815-c6893b97ea30.html.
———. "Railroads' Arrival in 1853 Momentous Event in City History." *Pantagraph*, May 18, 2008, B5.
———. "Thousands Lined Track to See Lincoln's Funeral Train." *Pantagraph*, April 27, 2008, B5.
Killey, M.A. "Illinois' Ice Age Legacy." Illinois State Geological Survey, Geoscience Education, Series 14, 2007.
Kilroy Was Here. "The Legends of 'Kilroy Was Here.'" www.kilroywashere.org/001-Pages/01-0KilroyLegends.html.
Kinder Morgan. www.kindermorgan.com/business/gas_pipelines.
Landis, Tim. "Internet Loss Halts Farmersville Wind Generator." *State Journal-Register*, July 3, 2009. www.sj-r.com/news/x631612812/Internet-loss-shuts-down-Farmersville-wind-generator.
Landmarks Illinois. www.landmarks.org/ten_4.htm.
Lane, Alice. "Dwight Illinois Fall Festival—Basset Waddle." Ezine Articles. www.ezinearticles.com/?Dwight-Illinois-Fall-Festival—Basset-Waddle&id=2493818.
Layton, Julia. "How Do Hybrids Utilize Eco-plastics?" How Stuff Works. www.auto.howstuffworks.com/under-the-hood/trends-innovations/hybrids-use-eco-plastics.htm/printable.
Legends of America. "Illinois Legends: Farm Country of Southern Illinois." www.legendsofamerica.com/il-edwardsville.html.
———. "Illinois Legends: McLean and Atlanta." www.legendsofamerica.com/IL-McLean.html.
Lincoln, Abraham. "Farewell Address in Springfield," February 11, 1861. National Center. www.nationalcenter.org/Lincoln%27sFarewell.html.
Lincoln Memorial Garden & Nature Center. www.lincolnmemorialgarden.org.
Linder Farm Network. www.linderfarmnetwork.com/index.cfm?show=10&mid=3&pid=1.
Lindsay, Vachel. "Abraham Lincoln Walks at Midnight." Poetry Foundation. www.poetryfoundation.org/archive/poem.html?id=176810.
Lithuanian World Center. www.lithuanianworldcenter.org.
Logan County Genealogical and Historical Society. www.rootsweb.ancestry.com/~illcghs.
Loomis, David G., PhD. "Economic Costs and Benefits of Wind Farms." East Central Illinois Economic Development District, January 30, 2009. www.eciedd.org/pdf/publications/ILWindWorkingGroup_Pres.pdf.

BIBLIOGRAPHY

Matejka, Mike. "Building a Railroad: 1850s Irish Immigrant Labor in Central Illinois." *Irish Immigrants in McLean County, Illinois*. Edited by Greg Koos. Bloomington, IL: McLean County Museum of History, 2000.
Mitsubishi Motors North America Inc. www.mitsubishimanufacturing.com.
National Agricultural Statistics Service. "Illinois." www.nass.usda.gov/Statistics_by_State/Illinois.
National Garden Clubs. "Blue Star Memorial Program." www.gardenclub.org/1345.
National Park Service. "Fencing the Great Plains: The History of Barbed Wire." www.nps.gov/home/planyourvisit/upload/Barbed%20Wire%20Brochure,%20final.pdf.
———. "Plant Conservation Alliance's Alien Plant Working Group Least Wanted: Common Reed." www.nps.gov/plants/alien/fact/phau1.htm.
National Remember Our Troops Campaign. "History and Current Status of: The Blue Star Memorial Highways." www.nrotc.org/blue.star.mem.hwy.htm.
National Weather Service. "Montgomery County, IL." www.crh.noaa.gov/lsx/?n=montgyil_tor.
New Spirit Inc. "History of Oil and Gas Production in Illinois." www.nsioil.com/oil-in-illinois.
Old Gillett Farm. "Edward's Trace Trail." www.oldgillettfarm.org/kentucky_house_tavern/edwards_trace.html.
150 Years of Blessings: St. Paul Lutheran Church. Hamel, IL: self-published, 2006.
Operation Lifesaver Inc. www.oli.org.
Owen, Mary. "Joliet Landmark: From Queen of Dairies to King of Kings." *Chicago Tribune*, November 21, 2010.
Parade. "How We Can Save Our Roads." www.parade.com/news/2009/03/how-we-can-save-our-roads.html?index=3.
Passic, Frank. "Lithuanian Lodge Tokens of Chicago." *The Numismatist*, May 1981. www.albionmich.com/history/histor_notebook/S_Lodge.shtml.
Paul Simon Public Policy Institute. "Paul Simon Biography: Institute Founder (1928–2003)." www.paulsimoninstitute.org/index.php?option=com_content&view=article&id=233&Itemid=197.
Phillips, Jan. *Wild Edibles of Missouri*. Jefferson City: Missouri Department of Conservation, 1998.
Prats, J.J., ed. "The Diamond Mine Disaster." Historical Marker Database, April 3, 2008. http://www.hmdb.org/marker.asp?marker=6868.
Reck, Don. "Springfieldian Scuttled Sangamo Town's Plans." *Illinois State Journal*, February 9, 1960, 1-2.

Bibliography

Reinhart, Josh. "Heartland's WDC Earns Prestigious LEED® Green Building Certification." Capital Development Board. October 28, 2009. www.cdb.state.il.us/forms/download/HeartlandLEED.pdf.

Republic Services. "Landfills." www.alliedwastechicago.com/landfills.

Reynolds, John. "Erin's Pavilion Opens Today at Southwind Park." *State Journal-Register*. May 19, 2010. www.sj-r.com/carousel/x1560867537/Erin-s-pavilion-opens-today-at-Southwind-Park?photo=0.

Richardson, Scott. "100 Year Later, Tragedy of Cherry Mine Disaster Still Hits Home." *Pantagraph*, April 11, 2009. www.pantagraph.com/news/article_837d60e3-7dd8-556c-b595-0a7fdaac7b5b.html.

Roadside America. "Lincoln, Illinois: World's Largest Wagon and Big Lincoln." www.roadsideamerica.com/tip/7692.

The Road Wanderer. "Funks Grove and the Dixie Truckers Home." www.theroadwanderer.net/66Illinois/funks.htm.

———. "Illinois Route 66." www.theroadwanderer.net/66Illinois/route66IL.htm.

Robertson, Kenneth R. "Planning With Plants in Illinois." Illinois Natural History Survey. www.inhs.illinois.edu/animals_plants/prairie/plants/planningplants.html.

Russo, Edward J. *Prairie of Promise: Springfield and Sangamon County*. Woodland Hills, CA: Windsor Publications, 1983.

Salt Institute. www.saltinstitute.org.

Sangamon County Historical Society. www.sancohis.org.

Sangamon County, Illinois. www.co.sangamon.il.us/History/default.asp.

Sangamo town map. *Journal of the Illinois State Historical Society 19* (1926): 3–4. www.jstor.org/pss/40187558.

Sapochetti, Tony. "Open House Gives Up-Close Look at Livingston Landfill." *Pantagraph*, August 7, 2009. www.pantagraph.com/news/local/article_77a5e786-839d-11de-adbc-001cc4c002e0.html.

Schmeekle Reserve Interpreters. "Illinois Historic Route 66 Master Interpretive Plan." May 2008. www.uwsp.edu/cnr/Schmeeckle/Consulting/docs/Ill_rt66_IMP.pdf.

School of Biological Sciences, Illinois State University. www.bio.ilstu.edu.

Seppa, Nathan. "Metropolitan Life on the Mississippi." *Washington Post*. March 12, 1997. www.washingtonpost.com/wp-srv/national/daily/march/12/cahokia.htm.

Shurtleff, William, and Akiko Aoyagi. "Henry Ford and His Employees: Work With Soy." Soy Info Center, 2004. www.soyinfocenter.com/HSS/henry_ford_and_employees.php.

Bibliography

Sipple, Kim. "The History of Coal City." Village of Coal City. www.coalcity-il.com/history.
Southern Illinoisan. "Parthenon on the Sangamon? State's $12 Million Building Is Hot Political Issue." May 31, 1968.
Southwind Park. Springfield, Illinois. www.southwindpark.org/home.asp.
Soybean Meal INFOcenter. soymeal.org/pdf/HistorySoybeanUse.pdf.
St. Paul Lutheran Church UAC. www.stpaullutheranchurchhamel.org.
State of Illinois. "Governor Pat Quinn." http://www2.illinois.gov/gov/Pages/default.aspx.
———. *Welcome to the Illinois State Capitol.* Pamphlet. Springfield, IL: self-published, April 2007.
State of Illinois Department of Agriculture. "Facts About Illinois Agriculture." www.agr.state.il.us/about/agfacts.html.
Steinbeck, John. *The Grapes of Wrath.* New York: Penguin Books, 1976.
Stringer, Lawrence B. "History of Atlanta, IL." *History of Logan County, Illinois.* Chicago: Pioneer Publishing Company, 1911. http://history.rays-place.com/il/logan-atlanta.htm.
Towanda Area Historical Society. www.towandahistory.org.
Town of Normal. www.normal.org/About/History.asp.
Traditional Music Library. "The Death of Mother Jones." www.traditionalmusic.co.uk/song-midis/Death_of_Mother_Jones.htm.
Truck Centers Inc. www.truckcentersinc.com.
United Soybean Board. www.unitedsoybean.org.
United States Department of Energy. www.eia.gov.
United States Department of Federal Affairs. "Abraham Lincoln National Cemetery." http://www.cem.va.gov/CEMs/nchp/abrahamlincoln.asp.
United States Energy Information Administration. "Coal Production and Number of Mines by State and Mine Type, 2011, 2010." www.eia.gov/coal/annual/pdf/table1.pdf.
United States Forest Service. www.fs.fed.us.
United States Mine Rescue Association. "Historical Data on Mine Disasters in the United States." www.usmra.com/saxsewell/historical.htm.
Upper Limits. www.upperlimits.com.
Valente, Judith. *Discovering Moons.* Virtual Artist Collective, 2009.
Village of Glen Carbon. www.glen-carbon.il.us/index.aspx.
Village of Romeoville. www.romeoville.org/history.aspx.
Village of Sherman. www.shermanil.org.
Vogel, Virgil J. *Indian Place Names in Illinois.* Pamphlet Series 4. Springfield: Illinois State Historical Society, 1963.

BIBLIOGRAPHY

Wade, Rick. "The View from Elkhart Hill: A Town of Enduring Character at the Crossroads of History." *Illinois Times*, March 18, 2009. www.illinoistimes.com/Springfield/article-5781-the-view-from-elkhart-hill.html.
Watts, May Theilgaard. *Reading the Landscape of America*. New York: Macmillan Publishing Company, 1975.
Waukesha Now. "What's in Those Cone-Shaped Buildings?" May 24, 2011. www.waukeshanow.com/news/122524639.html.
Whitaker, Steve et al. "Drilling for Oil in Illinois." Video, Illinois Petroleum Resources Board, 2006.
White Fence Farms. www.whitefencefarm-il.com/index.php.
Wilhoit, Robin. "Live Green at Heart: Illinois Wind Powers the Valley." WBIR, February 8, 2011. www.wbir.com/dontmiss/156301/207/Live-Green-at-Heart-Illinois-wind-powers-the-Valley.
Will County Historical Society. www.willcountyhistory.org.
Women in History. "'Mother' Mary Harris Jones Biography." Lakewood Public Library, updated March 4, 2013. www.lkwdpl.org/wihohio/jone-mar.htm.
World's Largest Catsup Bottle. www.catsupbottle.com/history.html.

INTERVIEWS

Albertson, Mark. Illinois Soybean Association, Bloomington, Illinois, February 13, 2013.
Banovic, Marilyn, and Ed Banovic. Owners of Honey Bend Herefords, Litchfield, Illinois, August 10, 2010.
Bolen, Bill, and Bonnie Bolen. Local residents, Odell, Illinois, August 17, 2010.
Boyd, Don. Viper Mine, Williamsville, Illinois, January 3, 2011, and August 7, 2012.
Carter, Harold. Owner of Carter's Nursery, Williamsville, Illinois, August 24, 2011.
Church, Dr. William. Professor of English at Missouri Western State University, Savannah, Missouri, January 17, 2011.
Cox, Joey. Farmer, Savannah, Missouri, January 20, 2011.
Crombie, Paul, Assistant Manager. Elkhart Grain Company, Elkhart, Illinois, April 13, 2011.
Dostal, Ray, Superintendent. Cargill, Bloomington, Illinois, September 9 and 10, 2010.

BIBLIOGRAPHY

Fear, Michael, General Manager. Springfield Hilton, Springfield, Illinois, July 2009.
Hammond, Dave. Owner of Pink Elephant Antique Mall, Benld, Illinois, February 26, 2010.
Hampton, Peggy. Local resident, Waggoner, Illinois, August 5, 2012.
Hetrick, Jeff. Public Affairs Officer, Commonwealth Edison, Ottawa, Illinois, September 26, 2011.
Hutchins, Marla. Local resident, Waggoner, Illinois, August 5, 2012.
Iseminger, William R., Assistant Site Manager/Public Relations. Cahokia Mounds State Historic Site, Collinsville, Illinois, June 6, 2011.
Johnson, Marc. Engineer, Burlington Northern Santa Fe Railroad, Rushville, Missouri. May 15, 2011.
Joyce, Richard (Dick). Local historian, Coal City, Illinois, August 6, 2012.
Kantner, Renea. Human Resources, Truck Centers Inc., Troy, Illinois, 2011.
Kauffman, Josh. Spokesman, Illinois Department of Transportation, Springfield, Illinois, 2011.
Kronmiller, Lindsey. Activities/Marketing Manager, Upper Limits, Bloomington, Illinois, June 2010.
Ladd, Geoff, Executive Director. Abraham Lincoln Tourism Bureau of Logan Company, Lincoln, Illinois, 2011.
Marten, Marlene. Local resident, Raymond, Illinois, August 8, 2012.
McCarty, Terrie. Happy Hearts Haven, Chenoa, Illinois, August 12, 2012.
McClendon, Wade. Conductor, Burlington Northern Santa Fe Railroad, St. Joseph, Missouri, May 2011.
Mertz, Joanie. Secretary, St. Paul Lutheran Church, Hamel, Illinois, February 26, 2010.
Miller, Catherine. Pre–Route 66 highway traveler, Springfield, Illinois, December 7, 2010.
Patel, Vinnie, Manager. Sun Motel, Braidwood, Illinois, March 3, 2010.
Perkins, Thomas H. Local resident, Gardner, Illinois, March 2, 2012.
Peterson, Sarah. Co-owner, Pontiac Flying Service, Pontiac, Illinois, March 28, 2011.
Sullivan, Diane. Owner of Duncan Manor, Bloomington, Illinois, October 23, 2010.
Trachsel, Kathy. Landowner, Chenoa, Illinois, August 11, 2012.
Waggoner, Jane. Local resident, Waggoner, Illinois, August 6, 2012.

INDEX

A

Abraham Lincoln National Cemetery 161
ALDI 44, 154
Allied Waste 48, 150
Alton 75, 76, 90, 129
American Bottom 97, 99, 102
Archer Daniels Midland Company (ADM) 67
Ariston Café 31
Armstrong, William E. 40
Atlanta 61, 62, 137

B

Banovic, Ed 84, 115
Barn Again 153
barns
 Meramec Caverns 47, 93
 red 107
 round 51, 52
beef. *See* cows
Benld 111
billboards 87
biodiesel 57, 58
birds
 American kestrel 140, 141
 Canada geese 158
 pigeon 89
 red-winged blackbird 92
Blackburn College 116
Bloomington 55, 56, 57, 58, 59, 60, 133, 138, 140, 150
Blue Star Memorial Highway 107, 108
Bolen, Robert S. 47
Braidwood 38, 40
Braidwood Nuclear Power Plant 40
Bridgeport 27
Broadwell 66, 67, 132
Broadwell, Charles 127
Broadwell, William 132
Bronzeville 27, 171
Brown, James 147
Brunnworth, Oscar 108
Brush, Charles F. 46
Bungalow Belt 27
Burnham, Daniel 172

C

Cahokia Mounds State Historic Site 95, 96, 100
Candy, John 40, 156
Capshaw, Kate 82
Cargill 57, 85, 143
Carter, Harold 129

Index

cattails 53, 54
Chenoa 50, 51
Chicago 172
Chicago Sanitary and Ship Canal 29, 36, 168
chicory 50
Chief Pontiac 150
Chinatown 27, 171
City, Water, Light and Power (CWLP) 72, 120, 124, 131
Cloud Appreciation Society 66
clouds 51, 65, 66, 117
coal 38, 39, 40, 73, 76, 80, 85, 88, 130, 131
Coal City 38
Coliseum ballroom 111
Collinsville 103
Conestoga 64, 65
corn 41, 73, 84, 86, 102, 118
counties
  Cook 167
  DuPage 29, 165
  Grundy 40, 41
  Livingston 149
  Logan 131
  Madison 12, 13, 89, 103
  McLean 135, 137
  Montgomery 114
  Sangamon 68, 122, 126
  Will 163, 164
cows 41, 84, 148
Coyne, Dale 32
cupola 146

D

Dairy Queen 162
Dale Coyne Racing 32
Dana, Charles 26
Demuzio, Senator Vince 117
Des Plaines Conservation Area 157
Diamond 38, 39
Dill, Lester B. 93
distribution facilities 164
Divernon 121

Dixie Truckers Home 138, 139
Dominion Resources 76
Dorsey, Benjamin L. 111
Douglas, Stephen 62, 132
Duncan Manor 55
Duncan, William R. 55
Du Sable, Jean Baptiste Point 25
Dwight 153, 154
Dwight, Henry 154

E

Edwards, Dr. Benjamin Franklin 75
Edwards, Ernie 66
Edwards, Governor Ninian 93, 105, 132
Edwards Trace 11, 105, 107
Edwardsville 95, 105, 106
Edwin Watts Southwind Park 74
Eisiminger, Jacob 132
Elkhart 68, 105, 131, 132, 137
Elkhart Grain Company 67, 132
Elzea, Erin 74
Exelon 40
ExxonMobil 160

F

Faultless Milling Company 63, 135
Federal Express Freight Center 65
Fell, Jesse 54, 60, 150
fences
  barbed wire 41, 42
  snow 44, 45
Fischer, Carl 163
Ford, Henry 141, 142
Ford Motor Company 142
Fronterra 35
Fuller, Thomas 129
Funk, Isaac 59, 140
Funks Grove 59
Futuro House 109, 110

G

Gardner 155
Gardner, Henry A. 155

Index

Geske, John 138
Gillespie, Joseph 13
Glen Carbon 94
Glen Carbon Trail 94
Glidden, Joseph 42
Gob Knob turbine 80
grain
  bins 54
  elevators 63, 67, 85, 137, 146, 151
Grant's Creek Nature Preserve 159
Grapes of Wrath, The 83
Great Chicago Fire of 1871 25, 171
Gridley, Asahel 147
Guardian Angel Bassett Rescue Inc. 154

H

Hammond, Dave 90, 91
Hampton, Peggy 80
Happy Hearts Haven 149
Harvestore (silo) 47, 48
Harvey, Paul 119
Heartland Community College 145
Hesse, Hermann 112
Hilton hotel 124
Historic National Road 94, 103
Honey Bend Herefords 84
Houbolt, John 34
House of the Future. *See* Futuro House

I

Iberdrola Renewables, LLC 151
Illinois Department of Transportation 42, 61, 125
Illinois & Michigan Canal 28, 35
Illinois Pork Producers Association 74
Illinois State University 52, 56, 144, 147
Illinois Wesleyan University 56
Interstate 80 35
Irish railworkers memorial 59, 60

J

Jacobshagen, Keith 7
Jefferson National Expansion Memorial 95

Jensen, Jens 75
Johnson, Marc 85
Joliet 34, 160, 162
Joliet Army Ammunition Plant 160
Joliet, Louis 31, 34, 90
Jones, "Mother" Mary Harris 88
J.W. Hawes Grain Elevator Museum 137

K

Kathryn Beich plant 57, 58
Keeley Institute 154
Keeley, Leslie 154
Kerner, Governor Otto 133, 134
Kilmer, Joyce 87
Kilroy, James 113
Kincaid Junction Power Plant 43, 76

L

LaGROU 165
lakes
  Lorenz 125
  Michigan 25, 26, 168
  Sangchris 76
  Springfield 73, 75, 107, 123
Lawndale 63, 135, 136
Leopold, Aldo 130
Lexington 147
Lincoln 63, 64, 65
Lincoln, Abraham 62, 63, 64, 68, 69, 70, 71, 75, 122, 123, 127, 128, 131, 132, 161, 163
Lincoln College 63
Lincoln Highway 163, 164
Lincoln Memorial Garden 74, 75
Lindsay, Vachel 122
Litchfield 82, 115
Lithuanian World Center 30
Livingston, Edward 149
Lockport 31
Loders Croklaan 37
Logan, Dr. John 131
Lowe, Marlon 136
lunar module 34

INDEX

M

Maguire, Reverend John W.F. 88
Marine 93
Marquette, Jacques 34, 90
Marten, Loretta 82, 83
Marten, Marlene 82
Martin, Steve 156
McCarty, Terrie 149
McClendon, Wade 85
McCullough, J.F. 162
McDaniel, Bruce 15
McLean, John 137
Midewin National Tallgrass Prairie 161
milkweed 19, 20, 135
Mitsubishi Motors 56
Moll, Pastor John 91
Money Creek 54
Montgomery, Richard 114
moraine 137, 138

N

Nail, Myron "Penny" 82
Nash, Ogden 87
National Council of State Garden Clubs 107
National Gas Pipeline Company 162, 163
National Heritage Corridor 36
Native Americans 11, 38, 49, 102, 132, 150, 155
Nestlé 57, 58
Next Generation Radar (NEXRAD) 63
ninetieth meridian 102, 103
Normal 52, 56, 135, 140, 150

O

O'Leary, Catherine 26
Our Lady of the Highways 82

P

Palms Grill Café 31
Peoria 105, 133

Peterson, Sarah 48
Peterson, Scott 48
Phragmites 32, 136
piasa bird 89
Pig Hip Restaurant 66
pigs 74, 84
Pink Elephant Antique Mall 90, 109
Pioneer Hi-Bred Production Plant 83
Planes, Trains and Automobiles 156
ponds 46, 158
Pontiac 49, 150
Pontiac Flying Service 48
Pontiac RV 150
Pontiac Trail 12
pork. *See* pigs
Porter, William 127
power lines 43
prairie 7, 20, 21, 38, 51, 59, 61, 75, 91, 97, 108, 109, 159, 160, 161
Proust, Marcel 8
Pulaski, Casimir 28
Pulliam, Robert 68, 122
pump jack 77

Q

Quantum Foods 164, 165

R

railroads
 Alton & Sangamon 59, 129
 Chicago & Alton 55, 59, 60, 129, 135, 155
 Illinois Central 80, 85, 94
rest area 49, 50, 58, 59, 117
Reynolds, Governor John 68
rivers
 Chicago 25, 29, 168
 Des Plaines 29, 38, 168
 Illinois 36, 38
 Kankakee 37, 38
 Mackinaw 53
 Mississippi 36, 95, 97, 102
 Sangamon 111, 123, 127, 128
 Vermilion 49

Index

Roadway Weather Information System 115
Rob Roy 121
Romeoville 31, 32
Route 40 94, 103
Route 66 12, 31, 59, 61, 63, 66, 73, 82, 83, 108, 110, 111, 130, 133, 134, 135, 137, 138, 139, 140, 153, 165

S

salt (road) 42, 43
Sandburg, Carl 26, 51, 88, 170
Sangamo Town 127
Schmick, Chris 143, 144
Schmick, Pam 143
Scott, Sir Walter 121
Sherman 128
Sherman, David 128
Shirley 58
Simon, Senator Paul 94
sirup 139, 140
Six Mile School 135
sound walls 33, 34
soybeans 41, 57, 74, 75, 76, 141, 142
Spielberg, Steven 82
Springfield 59, 63, 68, 69, 70, 71, 72, 73, 75, 105, 107, 120, 122, 123, 124, 125, 126, 127, 128, 129, 131
State Bond Issue 4 (SBI 4) 12
state symbols
  big bluestem 20, 61
  blue violet 18, 19
  drummer silty clay loam 21
  Illinois state flag 15
  monarch butterfly 19, 20, 135
  northern cardinal 16, 17
  Tully monster 23
  white oak 21
Steinbeck, John 83
Stevenson, Adlai 132
Stevenson Expressway 167
Stevenson II, Governor Adlai 167
Stevenson, McLean 137

St. Louis 59, 60, 90, 95, 96, 97, 144
St. Paul Lutheran Church 91, 108
Sullivan, Diane 55
Sullivan, Louis 171
Sun Motel 156, 157

T

Talisman 127, 128
Tall Paul 137
Tarro, Dominic 111
Taylor, C.G. 86
Thomas, Lewis 79, 119
Thoreau, Henry David 92
tile drains 149
tornado 64, 117
Towanda 54, 135
trains. *See* railroads
trees
  bur oak 22
  eastern cottonwood 136
  Osage-orange 42, 79, 80
  smooth sumac 155
Truck Centers Inc. 104
Twain, Mark 26, 98

U

Union Grove Stock Farm 79
Union Miners Cemetery 88
United Mine Workers of America 84, 88
University of Illinois 51
Upper Limits 144

V

Valente, Judith 47
Viper Mine 73, 130, 131

W

Waggoner 80, 82
Waggoner, Elizabeth 81
Waggoner, George 81
Waldmire, Ed 73
Walters, J.P. 138
water tower 29, 30, 61, 103, 145

INDEX

Watterson Towers 144
Watts, May Theilgaard 22, 143
weather radar 63
wetland 32, 49, 96, 97, 99, 100
White Fence Farm 31
wildflowers 61, 74, 134, 135
Williamsville 69, 130
Willis Tower 168, 170
Willowbrook 29
wind farms 45, 80, 135, 151, 152
World War II 50, 57, 89, 107, 108, 113, 135, 142, 160
Wright, Frank Lloyd 75, 87

ABOUT THE AUTHORS

LUANN CADDEN is a native of Springfield and spent twenty-five years of her life in central Illinois. During weekly drives from Springfield to Normal, she reconciled herself with the landscape outside her car window. The expansive sunsets and sculptural field trees enriched her journeys to the town of her alma mater, Illinois State University, where she received her BS in English/writing. While a naturalist for the Missouri Department of Conservation, she wrote magazine and research articles and interpretive trail guides. She is a teacher, writer and certified interpretive guide and trainer with the National Association of Interpretation, the professional organization of those who communicate about cultural and natural heritage.

Lifeshots Photography.

About the Authors

TED T. CABLE is a professor of park management and conservation at Kansas State University. Before moving to Kansas, he spent more than twenty years living in the Chicago area. He has authored twelve books, several book chapters and scenic byway video scripts and more than two hundred articles and presentations about birds, nature interpretation and travel. His consulting and writing have taken him to all fifty states and more than thirty countries. He has received numerous university awards, as well as awards from the Environmental Protection Agency and the U.S. Department of Agriculture. In 1996, he received the Master of Interpretation Award from the National Association for Interpretation (NAI), and in 2000, he was named a fellow of NAI.

Photo by Gerry Snyder.

Together, Ted and LuAnn previously published *Driving Across Missouri: A Guide to I-70* with the University Press of Kansas.